Order this book online at www.trafford.com
or email orders@trafford.com

Most Trafford titles are also available at major online book retailers.

Note for Librarians: A cataloguing record for this book is available from Library
and Archives Canada at www.collectionscanada.ca/amicus/index-e.html

Printed in Victoria, BC, Canada.

ISBN: 978-1-4269-1709-7

Library of Congress Control Number: 2009936932

*Our mission is to efficiently provide the world's finest, most comprehensive book publishing
service, enabling every author to experience success. To find out how to publish your book, your
way, and have it available worldwide, visit us online at www.trafford.com*

Trafford rev. 9/30/2009

www.trafford.com

North America & international
toll-free: 1 888 232 4444 (USA & Canada)
phone: 250 383 6864 ◆ fax: 812 355 4082

SERPENT'S KISS

I searched all my years for the meanings of life. In my search I encountered many concepts and philosophies. I read the Scriptures, and at first did not comprehend the significance of the contents of the Bible. So I continued my search for the Wisdom of the Ancients. Looking for God in all the hidden places and under the stones. When I returned to the Bible again I was ready to learn to look and see. I came equipped with the tools of Reason.

Many older individuals said to me, "The Bible is full of lies. The Bible has been stripped of the truth." And while I agree that many things have been concealed, I must also recount the truths still there. Truths, which as you will see, reveal a secret I will share with you.

For this reason, I must agree that the Bible is a light that will guide and strengthen the true of heart and spirit.

To begin my discoveries of the hidden contents of the Bible, I must take you to ancient texts that existed before the Bible was recorded. In doing so, we encounter an individual known as Hermes Trismegistus, which translates to "Hermes the Three Times Great." Hermes Trismegistus was known to the Egyptians as Thothi, and in Nubia as Tehuti. During a medatatitive state, Hermes Trismegistus encounters the Great Dragon that seeks to explain the Mysteries to Hermes. This is a portion of what Hermes Trismegistus related of the Dragon's revelation:

Hermes Mercurius Trismegistus from *Historia Deorum.*

> "I Thy God am the Light and the Mind which were before substance was divided from spirit and darkness from Light. And the Word, which appeared as a pillar of flame out of the darkness, is the Son of God, born of the mystery of the Mind. The name of that Word is Reason. Reason is the offspring of Thought [Thoth] and Reason shall divide the Light from the darkness and establish truth in the midst of the waters.
>
> Understand O' Hermes, and meditate deeply upon the mystery. So it is, that Divine Light that dwells in the midst of mortal darkness and ignorance cannot divide them. The union of the world and mind precludes that mystery which is called Life. Learn deeply of the mind and its mystery, for therein lies the secrets of immortality."

The Dragon goes on to say, "The Word was Reason, and by the Reason of the Word invisible things were made manifest…The Word moving like a breath through space called forth the Fire by the friction of motion. Therefore, the Fire is called the Son of Striving. The Son of Striving thus formed the Seven Governors, the Spirits of the Planets, whose orbits bounded the world; and the Seven Governors controlled the world by the mysterious power called Destiny. Then the downward-turned and unreasoning elements brought forth creatures without Reason. Substance could not bestow Reason, for Reason had ascended out of it…" Then the Father – the Supreme Mind – being Light and Life, fashioned a glorious Universal Man in its own image, not an earthly man but a Heavenly Man dwelling in the Light of God. The Supreme Mind loved the Man it had fashioned and delivered to Him the control of the creations.

Man, too, willed to make things; for which, his Father granted permission.

The Seven Governors - spirits of the planets, of whose powers He partook – rejoiced and each gave Man a share of their own nature.

Heavenly Man longed to pierce the circumference of the Circles and understand the mystery of he who sat upon the Eternal Fire. So Heavenly Man stooped down and peeped through the Seven Harmonies and in breaking through the strength of the circles, made himself manifest to Nature. Heavenly Man beheld a shadow upon the Earth, and his likeness mirrored in the waters. The shadow and likeness were a reflection of him. Heavenly Man fell in love with his shadow and desired to descend into it. Coinciding with his desire, the Divine or intelligent aspect of man united itself with the unreasoning image. Nature, beholding the descent of Heavenly Man, wrapped herself about Man, and the two were mingled.

For this reason, man is a composite. Within him is the Heavenly Sky Man, immortal and beautiful; without, is nature, mortal, and destructible.

Suffering is a result of the immortal man's falling in love with his shadow and giving up reality to dwell in the mortal darkness of illusion. Being immortal the Heavenly Man has the powers of the Seven Governors, as well as Life, Light and the Word (reasoning). Yet being mortal, he is also controlled by the seven Rings, or spirits of the planets, around whose orbits the world was bound and controlled by the powers of fate and destiny.

Immortal man is hermaphrodite, and eternally watchful. He neither slumbers nor sleeps, and is governed by the Father.

Such is the mystery kept hidden to this day; for Nature, being mingled in marriage with the Sky Man, brought forth a wonder: seven beings who were male and female and upright of stature, each exemplifying the natures of the Seven Governors. These, O Hermes, are the Seven Races, Seven Species, and Seven Wheels.

Earth was the female element, and water the male. From fire and ether they received their spirits...they reproduced themselves out of themselves. At the end, the Knot of Destiny was untied by the will of God, and the bond of all things was loosened. Then all living creatures that had been hermaphroditical were separated according to dictates of Reason.

To the ignorant, the body is supreme and they are incapable of realizing the immortality that is within them. Knowing only the body, which is subject to death, they believe in death because they worship that substance which is the cause and reality of death. At death, the material body of man is returned to the elements from whence it came; and the invisible Heavenly Man ascends to the source from which he came, that is to say the Eight Spheres or Circles.

Senses, feelings, desires, and body passions are returned to the Seven Governors; whose natures in lower man destroy, but in Heavenly Man give life.

After the lower nature has returned, the higher nature struggles to regain its spiritual estate. It ascends the seven Rings upon which sit the Seven Governors and returns their lower powers to each. It does so in the following manner:

> First ring – The moon, to which is returned the ability to increase and diminish.
> Second ring – Mercury, to which is returned deceit and craftiness.
> Third ring – Venus, to which is returned lust and passions.
> Fourth ring – The Sun, to which is returned ambitions.
> Fifth ring – Mars, to which is returned rashness and profane boldness.
> Sixth ring – Jupiter, to which is returned sense of accumulations and riches.
> Seventh ring – Saturn at the gate of chaos, to which is returned falsehood and evil plotting.

The Dragon

Now let's examine the proper word for that which the serpent bestowed upon man. The definition of 'conscience' is the faculty of recognizing the distinction between right and wrong in regards to one's conduct.

The definition of moral is one associated with the judgment principles of right and wrong in relation to human action and character. It is the exhibit of goodness and correctness of character and behavior, as well as one's ability to conform to standards of what is right, wrong, or just in behavior.

The word moral is synonymous with the terms ethical, virtuous, and righteous. 'Ethical' approaches good conduct from a philosophical stand, stressing idealistic standards; 'virtuous' pertains to one's sexual continence; while 'righteous' emphasizes one's absence of guilt of wrongdoing, and implies uprightness.

The definition of 'soul' is the animating and vital principle in man; which contains faculties of thought, action, emotion, and moral nature. It is also a non-material substance and thus immortal.

'Mind' is defined as human consciousness that is manifested in thought, perception, feeling, will, memory, and imagination. It is the faculty of thinking, reasoning, and applying knowledge. Thus, mind is synonymous with what we consider soul; for it too is immaterial and thus immortal.

Therefore while the Soul contains the residence for one's moral nature, emotion and thought, the mind is a consciousness that communicates its will to us through these various parts of the Soul.

In understanding these terms, let us recount what the serpent had actually bestowed upon man. We know by definition that this was a conscience from which man could sit as a judge, for he now knew the differences between good and evil. From this ability man became moral, virtuous, and righteous.

All creatures have animal spirit. But only man has the faculties of the Souls from which mind can communicate its will. Some people say the conscience is the inner voice; thus, the voice of God. In understanding that mind is also termed God you can see how God communicates to us through the faculties of our Soul. This has been termed by some as the intuitive self. Intuition simply means the act or faculty of knowing without use of rational thought processes. To know, absent use of reason. Through intuition, basic universal truths are made known to the self; for the intuitive self is of the sublime mind, and is not material or tangible. It is an omniscient presence. The principle of Mentalism dictates that the universe is mental. Being a part of that universal truth, the mind transmits knowledge through our Soul's faculties. It is this unique ability that made man in the likeness of God; for within man, exist the very doors leading to God. Unlocking and opening the doors are the means to dwelling in the light of God, and becoming one with the omniscient and omnipotent sublime consciousness called mind. In this way, my father and I are one.

Recognize that this ability to become upright, righteous beings was not given to man by the Lord God but by the serpent, the Great Dragon and Most High God. He, is the Lord of the word called 'reason'.

While the basic truth was here all along, we could not know of the God Most High without using His word, reason. Without it, we remained in darkness serving the Demiurges who has stolen the praises due to the God Most High. Only with reason can you divide the light from the darkness and dwell in the light among the land of those who are able to see. To these people, they are alive. Spiritually awakened. To those whom have not divided, they remain in darkness and are blind, dead, and dumb to the true god. To them, they are zombies. The walking dead who continue to serve the wrong God. This is why in the Book of Matthew, 22:32, Jesus said, "God is not the God of the dead. He is the God of the living." Similarly, Daniel stated in the Book of Daniel, 12:1-3 that, "In the end of time…huge numbers of people who live dead in their graves would wake up. Some will rise up to life that will never end. Others to shame. Those whom are wise will shine like the brightness of the sky."

They will shine because in them dwells the light of God. Faith is the key to unlock the doors of the Soul. Beyond the door lay the all-seeing eye called 'mind', The God of the Light who shines with the light that gives life. Recall in the book of Matthew 6:22, Jesus said, "The eye is like a lamp for the body." Once you allow the mind to come in, you will shine in the Glory of God."

The Dragon and The Word

When we hear the Hermetic term, the WORD, it is a term that is not just used by Hermes Trismegistus; but it is also referenced in the Bible, though you may not have appreciated the true significance of the term. In the Book of John, 1:1-5 it states, "In the beginning, the Word was already there. The Word was with God and the Word was God. He was with God in the beginning. All things which were made, were made through Him. Nothing that has been made, was made without Him. Life was in Him, and that life was the light for all people."

This scripture illustrates to us the Hermetic text that stated, "…The word which appeared out of the darkness is the Son of God, born of the mystery of the mind. The name of the WORD is Reason..." Thus, when we substitute the term 'Reason' for 'Word' in the scripture of John we get "Reason was with God in the beginning, all things that were made, were made through Reason. Life exists in Reason and that life is the light for all people." This is an almost exact understanding of the opening of the Hermetic text. Therefore, under this interpretation, we are like Gods because of reason.

John further explains about reason in 1:8-18 stating, "The Word [Reason] was in the world that was made through Him. But the world did not recognize Him (Reason). He [Reason] came to his own people. But His [Reason's] people did not accept him. Some accepted Him, and believed in His name. He [Reason] gave them the right to become children of God. To be a child of God has nothing to do with human parents. Children of God are born because of what God does. The Word [Reason] became a human being. He made His home with us. We have seen His Glory. It is the Glory of the one and only Son. He came from the Father [Mind] and was full of grace and truth."

This is so obvious I should not have to explain any further. All of the answers are right here in front of you. Think of what John said, 'To be a child of God has nothing to do with sex or whom your parents are.' Why? Because being born here refers to being awakened from ignorance, and thus, born into the Light. Wherefore, children of God are born by being taught to use the conscience, intuition, and reason. In this way children of God are born because of what God does. In other words, because of the effects of mind over matter, and then based on what the reasoning powers make manifest in the physical world.

Reason is Truth, thus is light and life. It resurrects the dead from triple stages of darkness: blind, deaf, and dumb.

Using the Hermetic definition, reason is the Son of God...the offspring of thought. The very animating and vital principle in man, which contains the faculties of thought, is by definition: the Soul. As I have indicated previously, the mind transmits itself through the faculties of the Soul. If thought is one of the

Those who still do not understand have hardened hearts. In the Book of Matthew, Jesus said of you, "They look, but don't see. They listen, but they don't hear or understand" (13:13).

The Devil

If God is the sublime mind, the Light and Truth, then it follows that Satan is the total opposite. He is ignorance and darkness – the father of lies.

Now contemplate this: why was the Lord God in the Bible a liar? Why did he seek to keep man in ignorance? Meanwhile, the serpent, who we've been taught to despise, was the bearer of the Light and Truth? He was the one who raised man up from ignorance to be like gods. Who is it that we worship? Obviously not the very one who bestowed upon us the great gift of knowing the difference between good and evil. Not the one whose gift gave man a morality. Instead, it is the Lord, the Great Demiurges who waits at each turn to defeat the great works of Reason. Look for yourself. Go to the Book of Genesis 11:1-9, wherein it states, "The whole world had only one language. All people spoke it…they said to each other, 'Come, let's make bricks and bake them well'…Then they said, 'Let's build a city for ourselves. Let's build a tower that reaches the sky. We'll make a name for ourselves. Then we won't be scattered over the face of the whole earth.' But the Lord came down to see the city and the tower the people were building. The Lord said, 'They are one people. And all of them speak the same language. That is why they can do this. Now they will be able to do anything they plan to. Come, let us go down and mix up their language. Then they will not understand each other.' So the Lord scattered them over the whole Earth, and they stopped building the city. The Lord mixed up their language of the whole world there. That is why the city was named Babel."

Maciejowski Tower of Babel

This is an example of chaos and confusion. This was done solely to prevent man from having unity and peace. This is the very definition of devilishness and wickedness.

Do you know the difference between good and evil? Then how long will you ignore the God Most High, who created you in His likeness male and female?

You have strayed far from the correct path of reason and righteousness.

Did not Abraham worship the Lord God? Read then Genesis 15:12-13, which state, "As the sun was going down Abram fell into a deep sleep. A thick, terrible darkness covered him. Then the Lord said to him…"

Herein the Lord appeared in a terrible and thick darkness! Not in the Light. Our God Most High divides the light from the darkness, for He is the Light by which the blind see. Not the darkness, which is the home of the blind. Only Reason can divide such darkness and establish the truth in the midst of mortal darkness.

Let's further examine the message that was given to Abraham, that his people will enter Egypt and become slaves. That the Lord will punish Egypt, but the people of Israel will leave with all kinds of valuables. This implies a conspiracy beloved. If I tell you that in three years' time, you will have a car accident and describe the exact manner in which it will occur, then you would have ample notice to effect your outcome. Hence, if you still experienced the accident, then would it not be because you wanted it to occur. But why would Abraham want this to occur? Perhaps because he knew his people would carry away many valuable things. Or, because of the pact made between he and the Lord? The very pact that caused Abram to add '-ham' to the end of his name, thereby changing it to Abra-ham.

Let's consider this Covenant. Genesis 15:18-21 states in part, "I am giving this land to your children after you. It reaches from the river of Egypt to the great river Euphrates. It includes the land of the Kenites, Kenizzites, Kadmonites, Hittites, Perizzizites, and Rephaites. The Amorites, Canaanites, Girgashites, and Jebusites also live there."

All of this was considered the Fertile Crescent, the land of milk and honey. Egypt was called Mizriam, Ethiopia was called Cush. Present day Northern Africa was called Libya, which was termed as Put. And Canaan was always called Canaan, however these are all the children of Ham – the father of the Black Race. Genesis 10:15-18 says Canaan was the father of the Hittites, Jebusites, Amorites, and Girgashites, among others. Therefore, these were Canaanites – Black People. And as you will observe, this pact was a pact of genocide, worse than ever before known in history. For these people who were brutally slaughtered for their land were considered the sons of God. Which is also denoted as Nephilim or Giants.

What God would give permission to another group to slaughter men, women, and children and then steal their land? Surely not the God Most High.

Yet in churches we sing praises about the annihilation of our own race, the destruction of our own people, and the theft of their land and removal of their traditions and culture.

Giants

As we continue our review of the biblical text wherein Adam and Eve became like Gods, we begin to trace the followers of reasoning and their descendants, beginning with the story of Cain and Abel. It is important to review this story as a tale of two kingdoms, which came from Adam and Eve.

Genesis 4:2-7 states, "Cain was the first born. He worked the ground while his younger brother Abel was a shepherd."

Now consider this symbolically. To handle sheep requires little to no skill at all, only a keen and observant eye for predators. In contract, growing crops requires the skill of agriculture, which is the science of cultivating the soil to produce crops. It includes horticulture defined as the science of cultivating fruits, vegetables, flowers, and plants. Among the skills required, is knowledge of Genealogy, referring to the mixing of two different seeds to create new and improved strains of plants.

Now let us bear in mind that the Demiurges put a curse on the land. In Genesis 3:17-19 it states, "...I am putting a curse on the ground...All the days of your life you will have to work hard to get food from the ground. You will eat the plants of the field even though the ground produces thorns and thistles. You will have to work hard and sweat a lot to produce the foods you eat..."

Therefore, we can deduce from this curse that not only was Cain required to work hard, his kingdom was required to use reason in their attempts to make the land conform.

Also bear in mind that the Lord did not appreciate such craft. In the Book of Leviticus 19:19, the Lord commanded of the people of Israel, "Do not mix two kinds of seeds and then plant them in your fields." Why? Because doing so would inevitably produce new seeds from the plants containing the inherent characteristics of two separate and distinct plants. This was a science of cross breeding. A science that the Lord God wanted to keep secret.

Now after some time, Cain gathered some of the things he'd grown. He brought them as an offering to the Lord. Likewise, his younger brother Abel brought an offering containing the fattest parts of some of his lambs. They were the first-born males to their mothers. While the Lord was pleased with Abel and his offering, he was displeased with Cain and his offering (4:3-4).

It's important to emphasize that Cain and Abel were not worshipping the Lord by making such offerings. The Book of Genesis, 4:25-26 indicates that the people not begun to worship the Lord until after Cain had murdered Abel and Eve had given birth to a second child called Seth.

Rather, this was a ritual by which allegiance could be made to the Demiurges. We know this from other biblical texts. For example in Exodus 13:2, the Lord says to Moses, "Set apart for me the first-born in every family. The oldest son of the Israelite mother belongs to me. Every male animal born first to it's mother belongs to me." Furthermore, in Exodus 13:15 it indicates that because the Pharaoh was stubborn, the Lord killed every first-born male son and animal in Egypt. Which is why Moses sacrificed to the Lord every first-born male animal…"

In the story of Cain, Cain's presentation of plants and not animals was an implicit refusal to pledge his allegiance to the Lord, the Demiurges. He presented the plants that grow from the light of the sun - a symbol of his allegiance to the God Most High, the Light and Life. This is why the Demiurges was displeased with Cain's offering, yet satisfied with Abel's.

Abel murdered by his brother Cain. (Engraving based on a picture by Vanderwerf)

The offering was a symbol that the Lord was ruler over the material world; and thus, man and beast. Not man who had risen to God stature, but ignorant man who was ruled by the darkness of matter and lower beastly nature. Yet Cain, knowing the truth, was saddened by Abel's disloyalty to God Most High. Abel chose matter over mind! Animal nature over the intuitive and rational components that makes men like Gods. Thus, Cain killed Abel.

When Cain killed Abel, this represented both a physical and spiritual revelation. For in disobedience, Cain had conquered his lower animal spirit and proven his allegiance to the God Most High. Thus, reason prevailed over ignorance. Cain destroyed a young empire that had begun to sacrifice and devote themselves to the Lord.

Now the Lord having dominion over the Earth, put a curse on Cain. Exodus 13:11-12 read, "So I am putting a curse on you. I am driving you away from the ground…When you work the ground it will not produce its crops for you anymore. You will be a restless person who wanders around the Earth."

Thus the Demiurges drove Cain from the land. Now why does the Lord consistently impose curses that concern the material aspects of nature? Because the earth is matter, to which the Demiurges exercises dominion. Thus, his powers are that of nature and its forces.

Now being driven from the land. a gathering tribe whom are further plagued with agriculture difficulties would be forced to make great improvements in this field. With respect to this, Cain said, "You are punishing me more than I can take. You are driving me away. I will be hidden from you. I'll be a restless person who wanders around on the earth. And anyone who finds me will kill me."

This statement indicates that there were other people existing at the time of Cain and Abel. In contemplation of this, the Lord states, "No! Anyone who kills you will be paid back seven times." The Lord then put a mark on Cain's forehead so that anyone who found him would not kill him.

Much misinterpretation derives from this statement, however this mark was not a physical mark or blemish. Rather, it was a ritual that performed by Cain as a reminder of having divine spiritual conscience and consciousness. An example of this is provided in Exodus 13, wherein the Lord had required Moses to set apart every first-born child to him. The Lord said to them, "When you celebrate this day, it will be like a <u>mark on your hand</u>. It will be like a <u>reminder on your foreheads</u>." (13:9)

Further, the Lord states, "One day the sons of Israel will ask their parents why they sacrifice first-born lambs and buy back the first-born donkeys." In explanation the Lord indicates, "This day will be like <u>a mark on your hand</u>. It will be alike a sign on your forehead. It will remind you…" (Exodus 13:16)

Therefore, it is evident that the mark of Cain was not a physical blemish on the skin, but rather a ritualistic reminder that identified Cain as being beyond reproach and harassment. Moreover, in order for this ritual to be effective it would have had to be known and understood to others as meaning in no uncertain terms, "Hand off!" What, then, was this mark, we ask? It was the use of reasoning by which Cain's deeds would produce great works. Works, which others would recognize as a sign that Cain was not to be touched or harmed.

The story of Cain indicates that the left Eden, and lived east of Eden in the land of Nod. Therein, Cain worshiped the Sun under Beelsamen. What is interesting, is that history indicates the first people to use the symbol of the sun as an image of God Most High, the Light of the World, was the Black Race. In fact, under Egyptian philosophy, Amen was considered the Supreme Being. All of the other Egyptian deities were merely different variations and manifestations of Amen, even Ra. Ra was the deity represented as the sun. For the sun possesses the intrinsic self-rejuvenating, self-sustaining powers, and is the light for all existence. Thus, the Black Race, too, were called the Children of the Sun. The very root of Amen in the hieroglyphics means to veil or to hide. Which was a concept applied to the Sun. Thus the term Amen-Ra can be defined, the "hidden or concealed Light of Mankind." Which, as we have discussed, relates to the mind and reason – the soul that is concealed inside the tomb of flesh.

Correspondingly, the Bible indicates that Cain's descendants were the inventors of architecture, musical instruments and music, as well as other useful sciences. Indeed, Genesis 4:17-22 reveals Cain had given birth to a son whom he named Enoch. And Cain not only built an entire city, but also named it after his offspring. Remember, Cain was not a man, but a tribe of people. For common sense dictates that a mere man could not build a city alone. Through Cain's descendants, Jubal was the inventor of Geometry, and the first to build in stone and timber. Thus, the craft of masonry was invented. Jubal's brother was the inventor of music and the science of harmony. He was the ancestor of all who played the harp and flute. Thus, the science of rhythm and vibration was invented. Also from Cain's lineage came the art of working in metals, or 'tubal'. Thus, the sciences of metallurgy were born. Naamah, who was also from the line of Cain, invented the weaver's craft.

These facts bring us to one ultimate conclusion. The first civilization known to man was the Black Race, a people of Cain. Nod was Africa. The Bible refers to this people of Cain as the Giants, or Nephilim, and later as the descendents of Ham.

These are the very people who are being slaughtered in the Bible. They are being slaughtered because Cain remained true to the God Most High. As well, because the Lord created a new people to whom he shed adoration and worship. These were the people of Seth, and would constitute the people whom the Lord would favor, protect, and influence in the greatest conspiracy and genocide ever revealed.

The People of Seth

After the destruction of Abel, Adam, at the age of 130, had another son called Seth. Genesis 5:1-4 states, "When God created man, He made him His own likeness. He created them as a male and female. He blessed them and He called them man when they were created. When Adam was 130 years old, he had a son in his own likeness. He named him Seth. Adam lived 800 years after Seth was born. He also had other sons and daughters."

Seth was to take place of Abel because Cain had destroyed Abel (4:25).

We learn from this text that Seth was made in the likeness of Adam. This is a very important distinction that many overlook. Recall when God created man He did so by making man in His own likeness. In this way they had become like Gods. However, when Adam created Seth, he wasn't made in the likeness of God, but rather in the likeness of man. Rather like the original man, Adam.

Seth, therefore, was not the original man; but rather a manifestation and version of the original. It is this new group of people that are the subject of the Bible's adoration. They are the chosen people of the Demiurges, and it was then that they began to worship the Lord. The Bible states in no uncertain terms that, "When Seth was 105 years old, he became the father of Enosh. At that time, people began to worship the Lord" (4:26). Therefore, it was in the making of the people of Seth that the Demiurges was able to procure a following and become worshipped.

The lineage of the people of Seth is listed in Chapter 5 of Genesis, and indicates that Adam lived 930 years. Seth lived 912 years (5:8). When the nation of Seth was 894 years old, Adam died. Seth's offspring, Enosh, lived 905 years (5:11). From this kingdom came Kenan, who lived 910 years (5:14). At 70, Kenan had a son named Mahalel (5:12). Mahalel lived 895 years (5:17). His kingdom conceived Jared at 65. And the Kingdom of Jared existed 962 years (5:20). Yet, at 162 years old, the Kingdom of Jared bore Enoch (5:18). Indeed the Bible indicates that, "Enoch walked with God for 300 years after his son Methsuleah. Then he couldn't be found because God took him from this life."

Recall that Enoch was a kingdom or group of people. Thus the passage indicates that they walked with reason for 300 years after giving life to a different nation. The passage indicates that Enoch couldn't be found because God took him from this life. Yet Enoch did not die.

To understand this concept of Enoch, we must reference other texts. In the *Ethiopic Book of Enoch* it asserts that Enoch ascended through the seven heavens (uniquely similar to the Hermetic texts Seven Spheres), whereupon he saw God Most High sitting upon a throne, Enoch then went to the four corners of the Earth. In the North he saw a great and glorious device. In the West he saw three portals of Heaven from which blow hail, snow, cold, and frost. In the South, he saw through a portal of Heaven, from which blows dew and rain. In the East the stairs of Heaven pass and run their course. Going East he reaches the tree of knowledge. While going west he was shown the Tree of Life. To the west lay seven mountains and the throne with the fruit for The Select. In the north the angels went off to measure. Enoch states, "They'll bring ropes and measures to the righteous which shall reveal the secrets of the Earth.

In ancient Egyptian text and philosophies it was taught that a unique few were able to escape a mortal's fate by divine invitation. The dynastic Egyptians developed this privilege into a right attendant upon the Egyptian Pharaoh.

Egypt God Seth

Thus it is most likely that Enoch ascended by escaping the mortal's fate. He most likely unlocked the doors and ascended dwelling in the light of pure mind and spirit.

As Hebrews 11:5 indicates, "Enoch had faith so he was taken from this life. He did not die. He just count not be found. God had taken him away. Before God took him, Enoch was praised as one who pleased God. Without faith it isn't possible to please God. Those who come to God must first believe He exists. And they must believe he rewards those who look to him." For with faith, one holds the key to unlock the seven locked doors of the soul and ascend into the Light of God and behold His throne.

After Enoch ascended, his son Methuselah lived 969 years (5:27). At 187 the Kingdom had conceived the Kingdom of Lamech. Lamech lived 777 years (5:31), however at the age of 182 the Kingdom of Lamech gave birth to the Nation of Noah (5:28-29). When Noah was ?? Lamech considered Noah to be the "Comforter" (5:29).

When Noah was 500 years old he became the father of Shem, Ham, and Japeth (5:32). 100 years later, when he was 600 the flood came (Genesis 7:6). Noah lived 350 years after the flood. Thus, the Kingdom died at 950 (Genesis 9:28-29).

While the aforementioned passage implies that Ham too was a son of Noah, thus from the line of Seth, I ask that you remain patient. For all these things will be revealed in due time.

The main idea brought forth here is that Noah was born from the people of Seth about a century later. These were nations as previously discussed.

In retrospect, Jesus Christ too was like Enoch. For He had not died, but rather, according to Revelations 1:5, was the first to rise from the dead. Not a physical death, but from mortal darkness and ignorance, he raised up from the tomb of the flesh to be a living God.

Misconceptions

In order to expand deeper I must prepare the way. Which means it is necessary to explain to you certain misconceptions in the Biblical text concerning the Garden of Eden, the individuals mentioned in the Garden, its fruit, and the mysteries of the Kingdom of Heaven. In doing so it will give you the necessary understanding to comprehend the messages given in the Biblical text and the significance of the story told.

Eden

In Ezekiel 28:12-18 the Lord makes reference to a city called Tyre, and states, "You were a model of perfection. You were full of wisdom, perfect and beautiful. You were in Eden. It was my garden. All kinds of jewels decorated you: ruby, topaz, emeralds, chrysolite, onyx, jasper, sapphire, turquoise, and beryl. Your settings and mountings were made out of gold. On the day you were created, they were prepared. I appointed you to be like a <u>guardian cherub</u>. I anointed you for that purpose. You were on my Holy mountain. You walked among the gleaming jewels. Your conduct was without blame from the day you were created. But soon you began to sin. You traded with many nations. You harmed people everywhere, and you sinned. So I sent you away from my mountain in shame. Guardian cherub, I drove you away from among the gleaming jewels. You thought you were so handsome that it made your heart proud. You thought you were so glorious that it spoiled your wisdom. So I threw you down to the Earth. I made an example out of you in front of kings. Your many sins and dishonest trade polluted your temple..."

Indeed, this parallels the story of Adam. We know from historical fact and geography that Tyre was a town and an ancient Phoenician city port on the coast of Lebanon. These black people were called the originators of written language in the form of cuniform. After 1400 B.C., Tyre began to dominate the Mediterranean trade. It was famous for its silks and dyes, as well as its purples and reds. In later times, the Phoenicians sailed to North Africa, to what is termed Morocco, and established a city port there.

So we know that Tyre was not a person but a kingdom, nation, and tribe of people. And we also know that this kingdom had dwelled in the Garden of Eden. How could this be? First, we must erase all the lies we've been told about the Garden of Eden, because those lies make it impossible for the Bible to have been true.

The Bible tells us that, in Eden, this city was crowned with nine jewels. These tend to correspond to the jewels of the Zodiac; of which, three are missing. Other speculations term these jewels as coinciding to the nine planets. And yet another refers to them as the nine degrees of the Masonic Lodge, which are divided into three levels containing three degrees at each level: apprentice, fellow craftsman, and master mason. The structure of which is equivalent to what was termed the 'Blue Lodges'.

We also learn Tyre was a cherub. According to the Catholic Church teachings, the cherub was a winged Celestial being portrayed as a child with an innocent chubby, rosy face. The cherub is the second highest in rank of the nine categories of angels. In many depictions of the Garden of Eden we see angels at the entrance to the Garden with flaming swords. These then were the guardian cherubs. Hence we know that rather than having wings, Tyre was a nation of people who protected the secrets of the Garden.

Lastly, we know that Tyre was expelled from the Garden of Eden because it became proud. In Ezekiel 28:1-6, this pride was defined by references that Tyre's pride referred to the people of Tyre regarding themselves as gods. And because of this, the Lord sought to destroy them. Interestingly, this is the same thing that happened to Adam and Eve. If you recall, the Lord said, "Now, man has become like one of us..." Therefore, Tyre must have eaten the same fruit as Adam and Eve, for they too saw themselves as gods. What is very obvious, is that God calls man gods, the serpent acknowledges that Eve and Adam would be like gods, but the Lord considers this a sin. This should further demonstrate to you that the Lord and the God Most High are different. For God specifically stated as recorded in Psalms 82, "I said you are Gods! And you are children of The Most High...!"

Correspondingly, there is other text that supports the conclusion Eden was not a garden in the literal sense. In fact, Ezekiel offers support that it was an empire composed of several different kingdoms. 36:33-35 states, "...On that day I will settle you in towns again. Your broken down houses will be rebuilt. The dry and empty land will be farmed again. Everyone who passes through it will see that it is no longer empty. They will say this land was destroyed. Now it is like the Garden of Eden. The cities were full of broken-down buildings. They were destroyed and empty. But now they have high walls around them, and people live in them."

Thus, this comparison between Eden and this land implies Eden was an empire with high walls and great buildings wherein people lived.

Furthermore, in 27:23 we learn that Tyre had engaged in trade with Eden. The passage states, "City of Tyre...Haran, Canneh, and <u>Eden</u> did business with you. So did traders from Sheba, Assher, and Kilmad."

Therefore, this land of Eden had still existed when Tyre was Lebanon. It must have been an empire because it conducted in trade with one who had been apart of that empire but was cast out. Therefore it is important to know from whence the Phoenicians came, in order to trace them back to the Garden of Eden. The *New American Desk Encyclopedia Third Edition* indicates that the Phoenicians were originally called Canaanites. They founded Carthage and Utica and the Greeks became the inheritors of their outstanding cultural legacy. Therefore, based on this historical information, we can trace the origins of the Canaanite Phoenicians back to the Black Race under the bloodline of Ham.

The Fruit of Eden

Another interesting misconception is the fruit from the trees in Eden. What was given to Eve and Adam? Was it an apple, or orange? To truly understand this allegory, we must first contemplate the nature of the tree from which the fruit is born. For since a tree is known by its fruit; conversely, the fruit identifies the tree.

In the Book of Ezekiel, 31, a message from the Lord was sent to the Pharaoh of Egypt, Hophra, stating, "Who can be compared with your Majesty? Think about what happened to Assyria. Once it was like a cedar tree in Lebanon. It had beautiful branches...it grew very high...it grew higher than any other tree in the fields...it grew more limbs...its branches grew long...all of the great nations lived in its shade. Its spreading branches made it majestic and beautiful...the cedar trees in my garden were no match for it...no tree in my garden could match its beauty. I gave it many branches. They made it beautiful. All of the trees in my Garden of <u>Eden</u> were jealous of it...Assyria was like a cedar tree. But I brought it down to the grave. On that day I dried up the deep springs of water and covered them...I shut off its rich supply of water. Because of that, Lebanon was dressed in darkness as if it were clothes" (31:2-15).

Lucas Cranach's "Garden of Eden". The Yorck Project: 10.000 Meisterwerke der Malerei.

Herein, we see that the passage refers to Assyria and Lebanon (Tyre) as if they were trees; and the waters as if they were wisdom, knowledge, and understanding. Based on this understanding of parables, we can discern the allegoric text of Genesis and understand that the trees of the Garden of Eden were not merely trees but rather kingdoms. This is supported by the fact that the passage states all of the trees in the Garden of Eden were jealous of 'Assyria.' Further, references from the Book of Ezekiel indicate that Tyre in Lebanon was expelled from the Garden of Eden, and had once even been a part of the Garden of Eden (28:1-6).

Since this passage deals with Assyria, let's recount historical data about this kingdom. The Book of Genesis, 10:8-12 indicates that Cush (Ethiopia) was the father of Nimrod. As will be discussed later, this was not merely an individual, but a group of people – a tribe from Ethiopia. The Biblical text states Nimrod grew up to become a mighty hunter on the Earth…at first Nimrod's kingdoms were made up of Babylon, Erech, Akkad, and Calneh. Those cities were in the region of Babylonia. From that region, these people went to Assyria region where they built the great cities of Nineveh, Rehoboth Ir, and Calah; as well as Resen, which lies between Nineveh and Calah. Likewise, history tells us that around 3200 B.C. a Sumerian people migrated into southern Babylonia establishing what is considered the first major civilization. In the 24th Century B.C., North Babylon was conquered by a Semitic people who established the Kingdom of Akkad (Nimrod). History calls this founder, Sargon the Great (c. 2360-2305 B.C.). As we know, Sargon of Akkad also built great cities in Assyria. The Assyrians took their name from the first capitol city on the banks of the Tigris called Ashur, which also had been established by Sargon (Nimrod). These Assyrians also became known as the Chaldeans, defined as a caste of Egyptian astronomer priests. Under them, Southern Babylon was reconstructed after its fall.

Therefore, there is no doubt that the geographical regions indicated in Ezekiel 31 were kingdoms. How could a literal tree be jealous of a kingdom?

Correspondingly, in the Book of Daniel, 4:10-22, the Chaldean King, Nebuchadnezzar, had a dream of a tree standing in the middle of the land. It had grown to be large and strong. Its top touched the sky and it could be seen everywhere on Earth. Daniel translated this vision and stated this tree signified the King's Empire.

You may recall that we spoke of the Chaldeans being the Egyptian priests who dealt with Astrology. They were considered extremely wise and also were referred to by some writers as magicians. It is very interesting that this kingdom would be envisioned as sitting in the center of the earth. For the tree of forbidden knowledge, too, sat in the center of the Garden of Eden.

Conclusively, it is clear that all those who were wise in the Bible depicted the tree as a symbol of a kingdom, not a tree in the literal sense. Thus, the fruit from the kingdom would bear the seeds that are similar to the kingdom. If planted, it would create a similar kingdom. Rather, one based on the same concepts, philosophies, and system or laws. Thus, the fruit in the Garden of Eden was the knowledge, wisdom, and understanding of the kingdom from which it came.

In a similar manner, the American Bill of Rights originated in France. Thus, it can be said that America ate its fruit from such a tree as well. Likewise, the American system of Laws came from England. In fact, it can be clearly stated that the United States has eaten from many fruits in the forest.

As Jesus states in the Book of Matthew, 12:33, "If you make a tree good, its fruit will be good. If you make it bad, its fruit will be bad. Therefore, you can tell a tree by its fruit." In light of this, was the fruit given to Eve and Adam bad? Can you tell the difference between good and evil?

Names of Nations

Another misconception is that names used in the beginning of the Biblical text referred to individual people. We read statements that Adam lived 930 years or Noah lived 950 and know that these cannot be single individuals. What human being have you ever seen who lived over 150 years old? With all the advancement in technology that we have, it is still impossible. Use reason to separate the light from the darkness beloved.

These names refer to tribes or groups of people – a Nation. In this manner you can clearly comprehend how one may live to be 950 years old. For example, think of the United States of America. In this context, Europe lived 300 years and then gave birth to a daughter called Britain. When Britain was 600 years old, she gave birth to a daughter called America. When America was a young child, she and her mother fought violently. So America left home with the help of a young man named France.

A person not knowing history would assume this concerned individual people.

However, they do not understand that the Scandinavian tribes called Angles, Jutes, Saxons, and Normans were a Germanic people who conquered Europe and combined its many regions into a united group of kingdoms by the 10th Century A.D. By the 11th Century, they broke up into individual kingdoms, forming Europe, France, England, and Britain. Europeans (specifically, Spaniards) settled in America in early 1500 in Augustine, Florida. By the early 1600's, the English had settled in Virginia, Massachusetts, Maryland, Connecticut, and Pennsylvania. The French, Dutch and Swedish also settled in the United States. However, opposition to Britain's policies toward the 13 Colonies led to the Revolutionary War. At which time, the United States received aid from France. Therefore, the United States, born roughly in the 1600's, has lived approximately three thousand years. If we mark the birth of the United States form the time George Washington was appointed as the President in about 1789, we still reach approximately three thousand years that the United States has lived.

A Biblical example of this understanding can be obtained in the Book of Ezekiel chapter 23, wherein a message came to Ezekiel from the Lord about Samaria and Jerusalem. Now we all know that both Jerusalem and Samaria were cities. Indeed the name Samaritan refers to the people who inhabited this ancient district of Samaria. It was originally a non-Jewish colonist from Assyria. Yet the inhabitants intermarried with the Israelites and later accepted Jewish Torah. However, they were not socially accepted and therefore termed 'good Samaritans.' As for Jerusalem, it was originally a Black kingdom. And we know Assyria, where Samaia was also founded, was a Black kingdom. Founded by the people of Nimrod.

In Ezekiel 23 the Lord said, "…Son of man, once there were two women. They had the same mother. They became prostitutes in Egypt. They have been unfaithful to me since they were young. In that land they allowed their breasts to be touched. They permitted their virgin breasts to be kissed. The older sister was named Oholah. The younger was Oholibah. They belonged to me. Sons and daughters were born to them. Oholah stands for Samaria. And Oholibah stands for Jerusalem…" (23:2-4).

Correspondingly, Ezekiel 16:1-5 states Jerusalem's father was an Amorite and mother was a Hittite. Since both the Amorites and Hittites are also Black tribes, it is clear they did not give birth to a person in the literal sense. Nor does a nation of people have breasts. Therefore, we see that this was symbolic of innocence and corruption as well as the intermingling of ideas and cultures. Giving birth refers to the creation of a new nation from another, in the same manner as the United States from England and Britain.

These were not individual people. In light of this you must use the same reasoning when you read passages detailing the ages of Adam, Noah, etc. For when the Bible mentions Adam, Cain, Abel, Seth, Enoch, Noah, Ham, Canaan, Nimrod, etc., they were nations unto themselves.

This is why the Biblical text recounts that Noah lived 500 years then had three sons: Shem, Japeth, and Ham (Genesis 5:32). Now recall that the sons of Ham were Cush (Ethiopia), Mizriam (Egypt), Put (Libya, located in Northern Africa), and Canna (the regions of Tyre, Phoenicians, Babylonians, etc.). As you may be able to see, these were not names of individuals but rather of nations. Egypt is easily located on a map, as are Ethiopia and Libya.

I realize that Genesis 6:3 contains a statement that "My spirit will not struggle with man forever. He will die. He will have only 120 years to live until I judge him." Yet this does not refer to the lessening of man's life expectancy on Earth. Rather, it referred to the amount of time before the flood was due to come. You must read the passages in their entirety to gain the full understanding. Don't let people give you bits and pieces without an explanation of the context from which it is derived. This leads to misunderstanding.

The Threshing Floor and Mill

The Threshing Floor and Mill is almost forgotten entirely in its value. We tend to read about it, but overlook its significance in Biblical passages. So I take this time to reveal its hidden treasure.

Let us first recall what King Solomon said about Proverbs in the Book of Proverbs, 1:2-6. "Proverbs teach you wisdom…They help you understand wise sayings…They give understanding to childish people…What I'm teaching also helps you understand proverbs and stories. It helps you understand the sayings and riddles of those who are wise."

The definition of Proverb is a short saying in frequent and widespread use that expresses a well-known truth or fact.

In the Book of Matthew 13:24-30; 36-43 Jesus gave a parable of heaven and compared it to a mill and threshing floor. He states, "The Kingdom of Heaven is like a man who planted good seeds in his field. An enemy came at night and planted weeds among the wheat and went away. The wheat began to grow and form grain. At the same time weeds appeared in the fields, the owner's servants came to him and said, 'Sir, didn't you plant good seeds in your fields? Then where did the weeds come from?' 'An enemy did this!' the owner replied. The servants then asked the owner whether he wanted them to go and pull up all the weeds. 'No!' The owner answered. 'While you are pulling up the wheat weeds you might also pull up the wheat. Instead, let both grow together until harvest. At that time I'll tell the workers to first collect the weeds, tie them up in bundles to be burned. Then to gather the wheat, bring it into my storeroom.'"

In 13:37-43 Jesus explains this stating, "The one who planted the good seed is the son of man. The field is the world. The good seeds are the people who belong to the kingdom. The weeds are the evil people and the enemy who planted the weeds is the devil. The harvest is judgment day. The workers are the angels…On Judgment Day the son of many will send his angels. They will weed out of his kingdom everything that causes sin. They will also get rid of all who do evil…Then God's people will shine like the sun in their father's kingdom."

Let's review this a bit. The field is an allegory for the Earth. The seeds are good people who belong to the kingdom. Angels are skilled workers who weed out bad people from good. Therefore, the storeroom is the kingdom. For the seeds that were planted come out of the storeroom into the fields to be planted. Here, the son of man is both the owner of the field and the storeroom. Therefore, the son of man is by definition a lord. For lord means owner. If the field is the earth, then where on earth is the storeroom? This storeroom would be a threshing floor or mill. To adepts in the Mysteries, it is called the Lodge. It is where the good people are refined.

Cylinder-seal impression circa 4th millennium B.C from Arslantepe-Malatya (Turkey). The seal depicts a ceremonial threshing with threshing-sledge.

A mill is defined as a building equipped with machinery such as a millstone for grinding grain it processes raw materials into finishing products. It shapes, polishes, dresses, and finishes.

This is a great clue to truth. For if the mill dresses, it affords clothes tot hose who are naked or whose clothes are dirty. It shapes us, and polishes us into fine and upright people.

Threshing means to beat the stems and husks of grain or plants, to separate the grain or seeds from the straw. The threshing floor is the place where such is carried out.

Now can you imagine a place on Earth where this is done?

Let's recall the Book of Zechariah 3:1-9, wherein Zechariah had a vision. He envisioned the High Priest Jeshua standing in front of an angel of the Lord. Satan was standing to the right of Jeshua. He was there to bring charges against the High Priest. The Lord said to Satan, "May the Lord correct you! He has chosen Jerusalem so may be correct you! Isn't this man Jeshua like a burning stick pulled out of the fire?"

Jeshua stood in front of the angels wearing clothes that were very dirty. The angel spoke to those who were standing near him. He said, "Take his dirty clothes off." He said to Jeshua, "I have taken your sin away. I will put fine clothes on you." And added, "Put a clean turban on his head." So they did. And they dressed him while the angel of the Lord stood by. Then the angel spoke to Jeshua. He said the Lord Who Rules Over All says, "You must live the way I want you to. And you must do what I want you to do. Then you will rule in my temple…High Priest Jeshua, pay attention! I want you other priests who are sitting with Jeshua to listen also. All of you men are signs of things to come…"

Now let's review this concept of a threshing floor and mills in the book of Ecclesiastes 12:1-9, "Remember the one who created you. Remember him while you are still young. Think about him before your times of trouble come…That's when the sunlight will become dark. The Moon and the stars will also grow dark and the clouds will return after it rains. Remember your creator before those who guard the house tremble with old age. That when strong men will be bent over the women who grind grain will stop because there are so few of them left. Those who look through the windows won't be able to see very well. Remember your creator before the front doors are closed. That's when the sound of grinding will fade away…"

In the Book of Job, 5:23-27 it states, "You will make a covenant with the stones in the fields. They won't keep your crops from going…You will go down to the grave while you are still strong. You will be like a crop that is gathered at the right time. We have carefully studied all of those things and they are true. So pay attention to them. Apply them to yourself." Job 31:9-10 further states, "Suppose my heart has been tempted by a woman, or suppose I've prowled around my neighbor's door. Then may my wife grind another man's grain?..."

In Revelations 18:21-23 it states, "Then a mighty angel picked up a huge rock. It was the size of a large millstone. He threw it into the sea. Then he said that is how the great city of Babylon will be thrown down. Never again will it be found. The songs of musicians will never be heard in your again. Gone will be the music of the harp, flute, and trumpet. No worker of any kind will ever be found in you again. The sound of a millstone will never be heard in you again. The light of a lamp will never shine in you again."

Now we know that this place existed in Biblical times because of the Book of Ruth, 3:2-9, wherein Naomi speaks to her daughter-in-law Ruth about Boaz, the owner of the threshing floor. She says, "Tonight he'll be separating the straw form his barley on the threshing floor. So wash yourself. Put on perfume. Put your best clothes on. Then go down to the threshing floor, but do not let Boaz know you are there. Wait until he has finished eating and drinking. Notice where he lies down. Then go over and uncover his feet. Lie down at his feet. He'll tell you what to do." When Boaz woke up he thought no one must know that a woman came to the threshing floor (3:14).

The story has great significance for Boaz was a master mason. His name was even used as the name for one of the pillars in the Temple of God (1 Kings 7:21).

The Giants

We are now prepared to review the basic facts of the greatest story never told. Our first encounter with the people of Cain is given in Genesis 6:1-2, wherein it states, "Men began to increase their numbers on the Earth, and daughters were born to them. The sons of God saw that the daughters of men were beautiful. So they married any of them they chose."

Here we see the first distinction between the followers of God Most High and the followers of the Lord. Those who followed the God Most High were the sons of God (people of Cain). While those who followed the Lord, were the people of Seth. They were termed men and daughters of men.

Herein we learn that these sons of God married followers of the Lord. Verse 4 goes on to state, "The Nephilim were on the Earth in those days. That was when the sons of God went to the daughters of men and had children by them. The Nephilim (also called Giants) were the heroes of long ago. They were famous men. The Nephilim (Giants) were also on the Earth later on."

Some translations of the Bible replace the word Nephilim for Giants, but they still have the same meaning. Giants are defined as persons of extraordinary power, significance, and importance. Thus we can deduce that the Giants were a great people. They hold great significance and importance in the past. Much of the text concerning these individuals was removed to conceal who they were. But fragments still exist and they indicate that these Giants/Nephilim were the Black people long ago. They were sons of God. If you observe the ancient philosophies of the Black Race, you will see that they considered themselves Gods!

Furthermore, the term Sons of God was explained in Matthew 5:5 when Jesus stated, "Blessed are those whom make peace. They will be called the Sons of God." So we can deduce that these people were not only of great importance and significance but were men of peace.

As the story of Genesis continues, the Lord sees how bad the sins of man had become on the earth. All of the thoughts in their hearts were always directed towards evil. As a product of this, the Lord set out to destroy man and the Earth. This goal would be accomplished by bringing forth the Flood.

This story now leads us to the story of the nation called Noah. There are many versions of this story however. In the Bible we are informed in Genesis 6:11-22 that God, being pleased with Noah, instructs him to design a ship called the Ark. Through this alone, we know that Noah was a man of reason, for shipbuilding is not an easy task. It requires skill and mathematics, as well as science. Genesis 8:1-4 demonstrates that during the flood, God showed concern for Noah and caused the waters to reside.

Correspondingly, in the old Babylonian myth, all-powerful Marduk, who was a sun god, and creator of the earth and humans, fought against the watery chaos monster called Tiamat. In this story one god starts the flood and another god, after an epic battle with a sea monster, ends it.

In the epic of Atrahasis, composed during the old Babylonian period (1800-1600 B.C.), seven gods seized power and forced the remaining gods to provide food for them. The lesser gods grew restless, however, and rebelled. To quell the rebellion, Enki, the wisest of the seven gods, developed a plan to create human beings to do the gods' work for them. The humans then began to increase. The gods became dissatisfied with all the noise humans made, however, and eventually brought famine and plague to reduce their numbers. But Enki saved man. So the gods then sent a flood; at which time, Enki ordered one man, Atrahasis, to build and ark for himself and his family.

This story is very interesting as it parallels the creation of the people of Seth, which is revealed later on.

In the Hindu Avatara, Manu Vaivasvata was the founder of the human race. Vishnu first appeared as a fish, Matsya, in order to save Manu from certain drowning.

In the Sumerian tale, a large planet appeared in our solar system. The Sumerians called this planet Nibiru (Planet of the Crossing). The Babylonian name for it was Marduk. As Marduk passed by the outer planets it collided with a planet in our solar system called Tiamat, and split Tiamat in half. The shattering of Tiamat's lower part created the comets and asteroid belt of planetary debris that presently orbits Jupiter and Mars. And Tiamat's upper part, together with its chief satellite, was thrown into a new orbit and soon became the Earth and the Moon. Marduk remained intact, trapped in an elliptical orbit

Marduk and his dragon, from a Babylonian cylinder seal

around our Sun, and returns to the point where it collided with Tiamat (between Jupiter and Mars) once every 3,600 earth years. It was the planet of Marduk, therefore, that gave us the 12 planets of our solar system, including our sun, moon, and Marduk.

I know that some of these versions seem farfetched. They did to me, but they have some truth because they are accounted in the Bible. Examine the Book of Job, which contains several references to a sea monster. In 7:12, Job states to his friends, "Am I the Ocean, am I a sea monster? If I'm not, whey do you guard me so closely?" At chapter 26:12-13 Job states, "In [God's] wisdom he cut the sea monster Rahab to pieces…His hand wounded the serpent that glides through the sea."

Another use of this term is found in Ezekiel 32:2 wherein the Lord sends a message about the Pharaoh of Egypt, stating in part, "You are like a monster in the sea. You move around widely in your rivers…"

There is clearly some mention of a sea monster being cut to pieces in the

Bible. Thus, the tales may hold greater significance than we give them credit. Recount for example the Book of Isaiah, 51:9-10 wherein it states, "Wake up! Lord wake up! Dress your powerful arm with strength as if it were your clothes. Wake up! Just as you did in the past. Wake up as you did long ago. Didn't you cut Rahab to pieces? Didn't you stab that sea monster to death?"

Whatever events actually occurred bringing forth the flood and ending it, we know that Noah's ark came to rest on the Mountain of Ararat. The story continues, indicating at chapter 9:20-27 that "Noah was a man who worked the ground. He planted a vineyard and drank some of its wine. The wine made Noah drunk. He laid down inside his tent without any clothes on. At this point, Ham saw his father's naked body. Ham then went outside and told his two brothers, but Shem and Japeth took a piece of clothing. They laid it across their shoulders, and then they walked backward into the tent. They covered Noah's body. They turned their faces away. They did not want to see their father's naked body."

Now when Noah awoke from his drunkard sleep and found out what his youngest son, Ham, had done to him, he said, "May a curse be put upon Canaan. He will be the lowest of slaves to his brothers." Noah also said, "May Canaan be a slave to both Shem and Japeth."

Now most people say that this tale was one of homosexuality. This is a major blemish upon the entire Black Race, for Ham was the father of all Black Races today. Instead, there is far more to this story than has been simply revealed. Indeed, we must review symbolism and other Biblical texts to obtain the truth of this event. The truth of which will increase your understanding and bring you closer to the revelation of the Story of the Giants.

Noah Revisited

In the Biblical book of Wisdom, 14:6-7 Solomon stated, "This is how it was in ancient times. A proud race of Giants was dying away. The hope of the world escaped on such a boat under your guidance and left the world a new generation to carry on the human race. A blessing was on Noah's wooden boat that allowed righteousness to survive…"

Based on this text it is evident that the Nephilim were dying away. Which indicates that they were approximately five percent of the nation. The remaining populous was blind to the truth, worshipped a mystery, and evil in the sight of God the Most High. When God instructed Noah about the ark and inevitable flood, he also gave him something to carry along in the boat that would carry on righteousness in the new era. This blessing on Noah's boat was Ham.

Interestingly, Ham was not a true son of Noah, nor the biological brother of Shem and Japeth. We've already discussed that these names were not mere people, but nations or tribes.

But let's dig deeper for a second to illustrate this point further. If you recall, the Bible states that Noah bore Shem, Ham, and Japeth at the age of 500. Yet, Shem, Ham, and Japeth were not triplets. This means in one year he gave birth to three sons, at the age of 500! Clearly, this is not feasible.

Also recall that Noah was said to have been 600 when the flood came on earth (Genesis 7:6). This would have made Shem, Ham, and Japeth 100 years old when the flood came on earth since they were born when Noah was 500. However, Genesis 11:10 states that two years after the flood had ended, Shem was 100 years old. This indicates that two years earlier he was 98! Thus, he was 98 when the flood occurred, not 100. Thus, it is impossible for Shem to have been born when Noah was

500 years old. Especially since the flood occurred 100 years after he was supposedly born. This indicates a discrepancy in the birth records.

In Genesis 10:21 a very interesting statement is made that "...Shem was Japeth's younger brother..." This indicates Japeth was the oldest. Since Shem was the youngest and Japeth was the oldest, Ham would therefore have been in the middle. Yet, the passage makes no references to Ham, nor that Ham even had a brother. Instead, it indicates that only Shem and Japeth were biological brothers, for these two nations were descendants of the people of Seth. Thus, Ham would have to have been the blessing on the boat – the only Giant Race left.

This brings us to the mystery of Noah's nakedness. First realize, the concept of clothing and nakedness is symbolic. It represented Noah's shame, not a sexual incident. To further understand this concept, let's review symbolism for a moment.

In the Book of Nahum, 3:5 it says, "'Nineveh, I am against you' announces the Lord who rules over all. 'I will pull your skirts up over your face. I will show the nations your naked body. Kingdoms will make fun of your shame.'"

Now, Nineveh was not a person or female, but rather a capitol city of Assyria on the Tigris River opposite the modern-day Mosul, Iraq. Nimrod, a descendant of Ham, built the city. Thus, nakedness was not a sexual reference.

In Revelations 3:17-18, references were made to Laodicea, one of the seven churches in Greece. It reads, "You are poor, blind, and naked...Buy from me white clothes to wear. Then you will be able to cover your shameful nakedness." This too was not a person, but rather a church.

In Ezekiel 23, references were made to Jerusalem and Samaria, referring to them as sisters named Oholah, and Oholibah. Verse 5 states, "Oholah was unfaithful. She longed for Assyrian lovers...They stripped her naked." As for Oholibah, verse 18 states she acted like a prostitute who had no shame at all. "She openly showed her naked body..." In verse 29 it states, "Of these two nations...They will take everything you worked for away from you. They will leave you naked and bare. Then everyone will see you are a prostitute who has no shame at all."

Since these were actually nations, the references of being naked were therefore not literal but allegorical. Let's review how to use these symbols in order to gain greater understanding.

In Job 31:26 Job says, "Suppose I've worshipped the sun in all of its glory. I've bowed down to the moon in all of its beauty." Let's now forever associate beauty with the moon and glory with the sun. These are symbols we can now use, as well as understand their significance when used by others. They can describe the type of person someone appears to be, your clothes, your appearance, etc.

For example, in Job 40:10 the Lord states, "...Put on your glory and beauty as if they were your clothes. Also put honor and majesty on."

And in Isiah 51:9, "...Dress your powerful arm with strength as if it were your clothes."

With these concepts of clothing in mind, analyze the statement in Revelations 12:1 wherein it states, "A great and miraculous sign appeared in Heaven. It was a woman wearing the sun like clothes. The moon was under her feet. On her head she wore a crown of twelve stars."

Based on the symbolism, we can interpret this statement to mean that the woman was dressed in glory, splendor, and greatness. This was her image and appearance, and the foundation upon which she stood was beautiful. Of course we know that a person cannot literally wear the sun; therefore, understanding that these are symbols of something else, allows you to understand how wise men speak to other wise men.

Additional examples of the symbolic reference to clothing include Isaiah 50:3 wherein the Lord states, "I make the sky turn dark. It looks as if it is dressed in dark clothes." If the sky was dressed in black clothes, we know that this means it appears as night.

And Zechariah 6:13, "…He will be dressed in majesty as if it were his royal robe…" We know that you cannot actually wear majesty because it is not tangible; hence, the reference is an allegory referring to the greatness and splendor of rulers' royal dignity, splendor, magnificence, or grandeur in appearance, style, or character. In other words, symbolic of merely the *image* one personifies. That is the meaning of clothes.

In Ephesians 6:14-17 we encounter symbolism of God's armor. It isn't real metal armor; rather, it states, "…Put the belt of truth around your waist…Put…Godliness on your chest…Pick up the shield of faith…Put on the helmet of salvation and take the sword of the Holy Spirit. The Sword is God's word [reason]."

Clothes are Godly attributes that define us as having strength, wisdom, beauty, glory, majesty, and truth. A person without clothes lacks the qualities accumulated by one who has done great works and lived righteously. This is shameful, for it exposes them as lacking. They appear as a child or dead. For as Job stated, you come into the world naked and you leave naked. Those are the only times you lack clothes. To be a child is to be dependent and young in wisdom. Conversely, if people are evil, they too possess clothes. But in those instances their clothes are considered dirty. This is illustrated in Zechariah 3:1-3 where Satan brought charges against the Priest Jeshua who was said to be wearing dirty clothes. But the Lord gave Jeshua new clothes and in so doing, removed Jeshua's past sins.

Let us consider using glory and majesty in symbolism. In Job 24:6-8 it states, "The poor go to fields and get a little grain. They gather up what is left in the vineyards of sinners. The poor don't have any clothes so they spend the night naked." This indicates that that the poor lack the clothes of glory and majesty.

Consider Job 26:6, which states, "Death is naked in the sight of God…" What is death?

It is symbolic to ignorance and mortal darkness. Thus, there is no glory, wisdom, or strength in ignorance. It is naked. This is why Jesus said, "God is not the God of the dead. He is the God of the living" (Matthew 22:32). He also said, "Follow me and let the dead bury their own dead" (Matthew 8:22).

Finally, consider Job 27:16-17, where Job says, "Sinners store up silver like dust and clothes like piles of clay, but people who do what is right will wear those clothes. Please who haven't done anything wrong will divide up that silver." This demonstrates that the rich accumulate wealth only, but do not wear the clothes of nobility, kindness, and generosity. And is why Jesus said "It will be easier for a camel to go through the eye of a needle than for the rich to enter the Kingdom of Heaven."

Now what causes us shame? Ignorance. In Isaiah 44:9 it states, "…They don't know anything so they will be put to shame."

Based on this understanding, you can discern completely that Noah's nakedness was symbolic. Ham attempted to show this nakedness to Shem and Japeth. However, when Ham called upon Shem and Japeth to behold that Noah was void of any glory, Shem and Japeth covered it up. They did not want to acknowledge the truth so they turned their back on the truth that the nation of Noah lacked majesty, glory, wisdom, and beauty. It had fallen asleep from its own self-induced intoxication. This was shameful conduct for a righteous people. But Shem and Japeth concealed this fact, as seen by their walking backwards and placing a cover over Noah.

When Noah learned that his nakedness was seen by Ham and exposed, he did not curse Ham. Instead, he cursed Canaan. He did not curse Egypt, Ethiopia, or Libya – only Canaan, which was the youngest of the nations from Ham.

Noah proclaimed, "May Canaan be the slave of Shem. Shem is the descendent of the people of Seth associated with the people of the Bible called Israelites," who would later go on to kill Black men, women, and children from Canaan called Giants...as you will soon see.

"Noah Cursing Canaan" by French illustrator, Gustave Doré.

In addition, Noah said, "May God add land to Japeth's territories, may Japeth live in the tents of Shem, and may Canaan be their slave." The Nation of Japeth was the people of Seth associated with those residing in Europe. As history indicates, these individuals sought to increase their territories by traveling over the Caucus Mountains and conquering the Hamitic territories of India, where they enslaved the original inhabitants under a caste system. They then called the area the Cradle of the Aryan Civilization. They also would later invade Egypt, Ethiopia, and fight viciously with Libya in the Punic Wars with Hannibal, as well as penetrate deep into the African interior and take over territories in places such as South Africa.

Therefore, Noah's curse was a curse on the entire Black Race, solely because that nation was exposed as being unrighteous and naked.

People of Cain Revisited - The Plot

Genesis 10:6-20 outlines the genealogy of the people of Cain. It illustrates that Ham gave birth to four great nations: Cush (Ethiopia), Mizriam (Egypt), Put (Libya), and Canaan.

I want to highlight some facts here, because these facts are critical in knowing the people involved in the conspiracy. Egypt was the Father of the Philistines (10:13-14). Cush was the father of Nimrod (10:8). The Kingdom of Nimrod left Ethiopia and built great cities in Babylon and Assyria. Among the numerous sons of Canaan were Hittites, Amorites, Hivites, and Jebusites (10:15-18). The term Jebusite may not be familiar to you, however, they were the people of a place called Jebus. Jebus was later renamed Jerusalem. Therefore, these were the original inhabitants of Jerusalem. Jerusalem had several names that you will encounter, such as Jebus and Salem (when it was called Salem, which means peace). Melchizidek was the king and the high priest of the God Most High (Genesis 14:18-20).

The Jebusite Melchizedek's righteousness was accounted for in the New Testament and the Book of Hebrews, 5,7. In 7:2 it states, "Melchizedek means King of what is right. King of Salem means King of Peace." We know that he too was a son of God by the definition given to us by Jesus in the Book of

Matthew 5:9, which states, "Blessed are those who make peace. They will be called the sons of God." According to the statements regarding the sons of God being Nephilim and Giants of the Book of Genesis 6:2, 4, Melchizedek was a giant.

The Bible indicates that despite these peaceful Black people of Jebus being sons of Gods, the Israelites would later come and invade the land and slaughter massive numbers of Black families. The stolen land was then divided up among the tribes of Israel. However, the Book of Joshua 15:63 also indicates Judah could not drive out the Jebusites who were living in Jerusalem so they remain living there to this very day. This is collaborated by the Book of Judges 1:21, which states, "The people of Benjamin failed to drive out the Jebusites who were living in Jerusalem…"

In Judges 19:10-11 it indicates that Jebus was also called Jerusalem. Because it was a "Jebusite city…a city of peace which I had to show you because I don't want you to just take my word for it. Therefore, with your eyes you have witnessed that these people were not evil. They were adherents of the God Most High."

We know that Egypt too was a great nation of miraculous works.

Yet in Deuteronomy, Moses tells the people of Israel that the Lord requires them to kill everybody! These were Black men, women, and children. Your people being slaughtered! You know their bloodline.

Indeed Deuteronomy 20:16-17 says, "…Kill everything in those cities that breathes. Completely destroy them. Wipe out the Hittites, Amorites, Canaanites, Perizzites, Hivites, and Jebusites. That is what your Lord commanded you to do!"

In the Book of Jeremiah 47:4 it reads, "…I am about to destroy the Philistines. I will not leave anyone alive who came from the coasts of Crete."

When the Lord spoke to Moses in the desert he said, "Send some men to check out the land of Canaan" (13:1-2). Moses then sent out 12 men, a leader from each of the 12 tribes. He instructed them to scope out the land of Canaan, to see what kind of land there was, and to determine whether the Black people were strong or weak (13:16-19).

These 12 men went into the land and came to Hebron, also called Kiriath Arba. That is where Ahiman, Sheshai, and Talmai lived. This city of Hebron was built seven years before the City of Zoan in Egypt (13:22). There is no question that the Anakin were Giants. It is noted in the Book of Numbers 13:33 that Anak was from the family line of Arba (Joshua 15:13-14); which is why the true name for Hebron was Kiriath Arba, most likely named after the name of the family line (Joshua 14:15). Hebron was where many of the people who were considered Giants lived.

At the end of the 40-day scout, the 12 men returned to give Moses his report. The report they gave is contained in the Book of Numbers 13:25-29, 31-33, wherein it states in relevant parts, "…We went into the land you sent us to. It really does have plenty of milk and honey!...But the people who live there are powerful. Their cities have high walls around them, and they are very large. We even saw members of the family line of Anak there. The Amelikites live in the Negrev Desert. The Hittites, Jebusites, and Amorites live in the central hill country. The Canaanites live near the Mediterranean Sea (Tyre and Sidon). They also live along the Jordan River…We can't attack those people. They are stronger than we are…The land we checked out destroys those who live in it. All of the people we saw there are very big and tall (Giants). We saw the Nephilim (Giants) there. We seemed like grasshoppers in our own eyes. And that's how we seemed to them."

Why did they seem like grasshoppers? Not because these people were actually taller, but rather because they were more important and powerful. They were an important people who built great cities and developed the land well. Their intellect was mirrored in their works, thus they were a mighty people making these Israelites seem small in comparison to their accomplishments.

Similarly, Ethiopia (Cush) was described in the same manner. In Isaiah 18:2, 7, it states "Land is along the rivers of Cush. Its people send messages on the Nile River…Messengers hurry back home, go back to your people who are tall and have smooth skin. Everyone is afraid of them. They are warriors. Their language is different. Their land is divided up by rivers." (Interestingly, these four rivers that divide the land are the same rivers springing from the place called the Garden of Eden.)

The Philistines were also considered Giants. You may remember this obvious fact from a story concerning David and Goliath, wherein Goliath was called, "A Giant!" Goliath was also a Philistine (1 Samuel 17:4-51) and had a brother called a Giant – as were the sons of Rapha, who were all called Philistines (2 Samuel 21:19-22, 1 Chronicles 20:5-8).

Correspondingly, the Bible references an Egyptian man as a Giant (2 Samuel 23:21).

Therefore, there is no question that Giant, or Nephilim, was a term used to depict members of the Black Race.

To eliminate future confusion I want to point out other names that you will encounter such as Edomites, Moabites, Ammonites, Midianites, Amelikites, and Arameans. These were tribes of people that descended from Shem, the people of Seth. They settled among the Black peoples' empires and even married Black people. They worshipped their own gods, in their own manners, but their very existence among Black people is very important to understand why the Lord hated them as much as the Black Race. For they, like the Black Race, did not worship the Lord.

The Edomites represent the children of Esau. In the Book of Genesis, Abraham's son, Isaac, had twins by Rebekah whom she named Jacob and Esau (Genesis 25:21-26). When Esau was older he changed his name from Esau to Edom (Genesis 36:1, 8-9). Under the name Edom, Esau took wives from among the Black people of Canaan, such as the Hittites and Hivites. His offspring became known as Edomites. They were adherents to the true God, despite the secret plot that the Lord made with Esau to kill the Giants of Seir and take their land as his own (Deuteronomy 2:5, 2:12, 2:22-23). Once settled in Seir, Edom was loyal to the original people and God Most High. However, we must not forget their initial secret plotting with the Lord to destroy our beloved sons of God.

The Amalekites come from Edom as well. Edom had a grandson who was name Amalek. The descendants of Amalek were called Amalekites (1 Chronicles 1:35-36). They too fought alongside Black peoples against the Israelite invasion.

The Moabites and Ammonites are the inbred children of Lot. In the Book of Genesis 19:30-88, we read that Lot had two daughters, who had sex with him and became pregnant. The older daughter named her son Moab (19:37), while the younger daughter named her son Ben-Ammi, who became the father of the Ammonites (19:38). Since Lot was related to Abraham, the Moabites and Ammonites were from the bloodline of Shem. Yet they too fought against the Israelite invasion (2 Samuel 10:6-10) and had initially made a secret contract with the Lord to kill the Giants and steal their land (Deuteronomy 2:9-10, 17-21).

The Midianites are also from the line of Shem. The Book of 1 Chronicles 1:29-32 indicates Abraham's concubine named Keturah bore Abraham six sons, one of whom was Midian. The people of Midian are called Midianites. They too had settled peacefully among the Black people and were the descendants of Ishmael (Judges 8:24-26).

Ishmael was a son by Abraham's Black concubine from Egypt (Genesis 21:8-20). Ishmael is the ancestor of the Muslim prophet Muhammad. Both the Midianites and Ishmaelites disliked the Israelites (Genesis 25:18). In fact, the Israelites had been instructed to kill all of the Midianites just as they would their enemies (25:16-18).

The Arameans, too, came from Shem. One of the sons of Shem was Aram (1 Chronicles 1:17). If you recall, Abraham's brother was Nahor (Genesis 11:26). Nahor's son was Bethuel (Genesis 24:2-47). Bethuel was the father of both Rebekah and Laban4 (24:29). They were called Arameans (Genesis 25:20, 28:2, 5). The Arameans too eventually fought against the Israelites (2 Samuel 8:6, 10:11, 17-19; 1 Chronicles 18:5-6, 19:17-19).

In familiarizing yourself with of all the figures involved in this tale, it is important to note that the Israelites were not the only people contracted to destroy the Black Race. The Lord had also secretly plotted with Edom, the Moabites, and Ammonites to carry out the same act the Israelites had done to the people of Canaan.

In fact, before the Israelites went to attack the Black people and steal their lands, the Lord had informed Moses that he was not the attack the Edomites, Moabites, or Ammonites for they were his relatives. He said, "Don't even anger them because they would go to war against Him" (Deuteronomy 2:4-9). Here it was made known that a secret pact that had been made with them to kill the Giants called Horites living in Seir (Deuteronomy 2:12). The Lord had revealed the similar pact with Moab to kill of the Giants called Emites. In fact Deuteronomy 2:10-11 states, "The Emites used to live there. They were strong people. There were large numbers of them and like the Anakites they too were thought of as Rephaites. But the Moabites had called them Emites." 2:17-19 goes on to state, "That land was also thought of as a land of the Rephaites. They used to live there but the Ammonites called them Zamzummites. The Rephaites were strong people. There were large numbers of them. They were as tall as the Anakites. The Lord destroyed the Rephaites to make room for the Ammonites. So the Ammonites drove them out and settled in the territory of the Rephaites."

The murdering of the Giants is also seen in the times of Abraham. In Genesis 14 we encounter the King of Elam, King Kedorlaomer. As you may recall, one of the sons of Shem was Elam (Genesis 10:22). Therefore, Kedorlaomer was a descendant of Shem. Genesis 14:5-7 states, "In the 14th year Kedorlaomer and the kings who helped him went to war. They won the battle against the Rephaites. They also won the battle against the Zuzites in Ham, and the Emites…They did the same thing to the Horites…They took the whole territory of the Amalekites and they also won the battle against the Amorites…" In fact, this very war was being waged around the time the Lord approached Abraham and made his deal with him to ensure his descendants possession of the land. I find it very interesting that as soon as the people of Elam attack the Giants, Abraham makes a pact with the Lord for portions of that land, then immediately thereafter, both the Edomites and Moabites make similar pacts to kill off the Giants and steal their territories. This is made less a coincidence, given the fact that all of these groups were from the family line of Shem.

Just imagine this conspiracy being plotted secretly behind the backs of the Black Nations. In Isaiah 43:3 it says to Israel, "…I will give up Egypt for you. I will give up Cush and Seba for you…" In 45:14 it says, "You will get everything Egypt produces. You will receive everything the people of Cush (Ethiopia) and the tall Sabeans get in trade. All of it will belong to you." In Ezekiel 32:7-8, it is written to the Pharaoh, "When I wipe you out I will cover the heavens, darken the stars, and cover the sun with a cloud. The moon will stop shining. I will darken all of the bright lights in the sky. I will bring darkness over your land."

Therefore, here is the underlying story of the Bible. An entire race denoted as sons of gods – Giants! – were being systematically targeted and killed for land, wealth, and because they did not worship the Lord. That is genocide!

The Genocide of a Black Culture

When the people of Israel finally came to attack the people of Canaan they first attacked two Amorite Kings (Joshua 8:10). First it was the Amorite king of Heshbon (Deuteronomy 2:24). When they attacked this Black city, they brutally slaughtered men, women, and children. No one was left alive. They also stole the cattle and anything else of worth from the towns (Deuteronomy 2:34). Next, they attacked the Amorite king of Bashan, named Og (Deuteronomy 3:1). King Og controlled 60 cities, all with high walls and city gates secured with heavy metals, which attests to the greatness of these Black cities. Yet the Israelites killed everyone therein, just as they had done to the Amorite king Sihon of Heshbon (Deuteronomy 3:3-7). Sadly, King Og had been on of the last Rephaites left on his family line. His bed was allegedly made of iron and was more than 13 feet long and six feet wide (Deuteronomy 3:11).

A large pole was driven through the bodies of these great Black kings and set upwards, with their bodies dangling lifelessly from it for all to see. They were left this way until sunset.

Through the Book of Joshua, this atrocity continues. This horrific slaughter and invasion persists, shattering the innocent lives of children and families – all in the name of the Lord. When the Muslims act in a manner similar to the Jews and call it Jihad, we say it is terrorism! Yet we praise these people for slaughtering the Black empires and first civilizations.

We sing songs of praises about these barbaric acts, praising the Lord. Why?

Through Joshua the Israelites attacked Ai. The total number of men, women, and children killed on that day was twelve thousand! (Joshua 8:25-26) The Hivites were so afraid of being slaughtered by the Israelites, they tricked the Israelites into making an oath that they would not kill them or their children. The Israelites instead made them all slaves! (Joshua 9:20-22)

When the King of Jerusalem, Adoni-Zedek, received the news that Joshua had destroyed Ai, and was killing Black people in such an atrocious way, he was furious. This method of killing Black people was utilized on the King of Ai and the King of Jericho as well (Joshua 10:1-2). Adoni-Zedek and the five Amorite kings ruled six great territories: Jerusalem, Hebron, Jarmuth, Lachish, and Eglon. They first set out to attack the Black Hivites who had made a treaty with the Israelite invaders to spare their lives. However Joshua and the Israelites surprised them with an ambush attack (Joshua 10:9). Many Blacks were slaughtered. The five Amorite kings escaped and hid in a cave. Joshua found them and killed them in the same atrocious manner. He cut the heads off of each king and struck them on a pole, and inserted another pole through each of their lifeless, beheaded bodies. He then stood the poles upwards, for all to see, and left them there until sunset. The beheading was an indication that in death these great people would be incapable of resurrecting themselves. This was a disrespectful thing in accordance with the philosophies of ancient Black rites of passage for the dead, as the dismemberment prevented the spiritual self from resurrection in the afterlife. In essence, the dead could never rise again.

The Israelites went on to kill the King of Makkedea and his people. Men, women, and children were slaughtered! He killed the king in the same manner that he'd killed all the other kings. No one was left alive (Joshua 10:29-30). After this, Joshua and the Israelites went to the city of Lachish and Libnah and destroyed the city and every living person in it. He then killed the Amorite king in the same manner as the other kings (Joshua 10:31-32). He did the same with the city of Elgon (10:34) and Hebron (10:36-37), and Debir (10:38). Everyone who breathed was killed! Not even a baby was left alive! (10:40) As a product of this first assault and invasion, the entire southern kingdom of Canaan came under Israel's control. He then set his sights on Northern Canaan.

After hearing of the Israelite's invasion and absolute annihilation of the Black people, King Jabin of Hazor immediately sent letters to kings all throughout the Land of Canaan. These messages were sent to the north, west, and east of Canaan. To the Amorites, Hittites, Perizzities, Jebusites, and Hivites. Outraged, the Black kings marched out together with all their troops. They brought horses and chariots along (Joshua 11:1-5).

Further, Joshua, being an excellent military tactician, did not attack this vast army straight away. Instead, he ambushed them in a surprise attack. This element of surprise led to his ultimate victory. He cut the legs off of the horses, burned the chariots and slaughtered Black warriors mercilessly. Those who fled were chased down and killed. No one was left alive (Joshua 11:7-9).

The Israelites then destroyed the City of Hazor, which had been the most important of all the Canaanites kingdoms. Joshua left no one alive. King Jabin was then killed in that special way. He then destroyed the city by burning it to the ground (Joshua 11:10-14). Joshua destroyed all the Black Anakites, who were considered great giants. There were not any Anakites left in the stolen territories, but a few had still remained alive in Gaza, Gath, and Ashodd (Joshua 11:21).

After Joshua died, the onslaught continued. The Israelite tribes of Judah and Simeon killed ten thousand Canaanites at Bezek (Judges 1:34). They also attacked Jerusalem and set it on fire. They killed the Black Jebusites with their swords (Judges 1:8-9). The Canaanite King Adoni Bezek managed to escape, but the tribe of Judah caught him. Judah 1:6-7 states, "…Then they cut off his thumbs and big toes. Adoni Bezek said in agony 'I cut off the thumbs and big toes of seventy kings. I made them pick up scraps under my table. Now the Lord has paid me back what I did to them.'"

The Canaanites living in Hebron, Kiriath Arba, were also slaughtered. And the Israelites then defeated the last of the Anakim Giants: the Sheshai, Ahiman, and Talmai (Judges 1:10), but these last three Anakim escaped (1:20). However, the Black Canaanites were again killed in the same atrocious manner at Zephath (Judges 1:17).

Despite this annihilation, the Israelites were unable to drive out all the Canaanites because the Canaanites made up their minds they would not leave their lands. However, when Israel regrouped and became stronger, they enslaved these people (Judges 1:27-33). This also occurred with the Jebusites (Judges 1:21) and the Amorites (Judges 1:34-36).

"Destruction of the Army of the Amorites" by Gustave Doré.

Even if we were to conclude that the Israelites were invading the land based on their faith in the Lord and their beliefs, it does not change the fact that this was genocide. In fact, when the Nazi's slaughtered the Jews over their beliefs, the world called it a Holocaust. It was condemned as a grave atrocity and reparations were made. Yet the Jews did not make the same reparations to the Black Race.

Today, if one group attacked another based on faith or beliefs, they would be considered criminals! It would constitute ethnic cleansing, terrorism, or like terms. Thus, when we review this story, it cannot be seen as anything but ethnic cleansing and terrorism.

Reason dictates that if the Lord was truly omnipotent, then he did not need the Israelites to kill Black men, women, and children, or steal their land. He could have simply taken away the breath of life for every living soul in Canaan that he deemed should be eliminated. The Israelites would then have only needed to enter the land and clear up all of the bodies. Truly this would have been a greater symbol of the Lord being the True God than a race of people running out of the desert killing innocent Black women and children, stealing their belongings and burning their cities.

The Ten Commandments that were given to Moses by the Lord state, "Thou shall not kill and thou shall not steal." There was evidently an exception to the rule when it came to Black people!

Interestingly, there have been no reparations made. To make matters worse, in 1947 the United Nations in Geneva Convention voted to divide the land of Palestine, which the Arabs had succeeded in taking away from Jerusalem. The territory of Palestine was divided between the Jews and Arabs and a new Israel was founded in May of 1948. Yet nobody thought to give any territory back to the original inhabitants of the land. This was not even thought of.

The Worship

It has been suggested in the Biblical text that the Israelite invasion was based on the will of the Lord, and their mission was to purge the land of sinful worship. Yet, what few seem to understand is that the ones who were purging the land of sin were the ones committing sinful worship. They were the worshipers of the Lord, The People of Seth.

This is evidenced in the Bible when the Ammonites entered the Black land of Canaan and worshiped a deity called Molech, to whom they sacrificed their children by means of burning them in a fire. They burned their children alive!

Similarly, the Moabites worshiped a deity called Chemosh, who was of the same nature as Baal. They also practiced human sacrifice.

The Midianites worshipped Baal and the sun, moon, and stars (Judges 8:21, 26). Which in all likelihood implies the Midianites practiced the ancient science of Astrology.

Accordingly, the people of Israel had done far worse than their own relatives. For example, a servant of the Lord, Jephthah, sacrificed his virgin daughter to the Lord and was honored for this (Judges 11:29-40).

Correspondingly, a Levite and his wife were travelling and stopped in an Israelite town, the Tribe of Benjamin. The men of the town wanted to have sex with him. The Levite sent out his wife and the men of Israel raped her all night long. She crawled back in the morning and died. The Levite then cut up her body into twelve separate pieces and sent a body part to each of the twelve tribes of Israel (Judges 19:1-29).

In addition, Israel worshipped idols such as a snake on a stick, which was possessed by Moses. They called this Nehushtan (2 Kings 18:4). They also worshipped the Goddess Asherah and bowed down to all the stars (2 Kings 17:16-17; 18:4; 21:3-7; 23:4-6).

Israelites placed male prostitutes in their temples (2 Kings 23:7). They also sacrificed their children in the fire of the Ammonite deity Molech (2 Kings 23:10). They set up chariots to honor the Sun (2 Kings 23:11), and they worshipped the Goddess Asherah and Molech (2 Kings 23:13-14).

Now what is very interesting is that this was the alleged Supreme Being who knows all. The Lord set these people of Seth apart for him and made pacts with them. Therefore it logically follows that the Lord should have known these people would enter the land and disobey him, and abandon him as their Lord.

Let us recall briefly the statements made by the Lord in regard to His chosen people. In the Book of Jeremiah, 4:22, the Lord states, "My people are foolish [Israel] they do not know me. They are children who have no sense at all. They are skilled in doing what is evil and do not know how to do good."

In 6:28-29, the Lord says, "[People of Israel] go around telling lies…All of them do very sinful things…It is impossible to make those people pure…"

In the Book of Jeremiah 8:8 the Lord says of Israel, "How can you people say we are wise? We have the Law of the Lord? Actually, the teachers of the Law have told lies about it. Their pens have not written what is true."

He continues in 9:3-4 and speaks to Jeremiah about Israel saying, "…Their mouths shoot out lies like arrows. They tell lies to gain power in the land. They go from one sin to another…Be on guard against your friends. Do not trust the members of our own family. Every one of them cheats…"

The people of Israel had seen God in the desert allegedly. Yet they still disobeyed him. Moses and Aaron disobeyed him. Even Solomon began to practice idol worship and other practices, and God gave him Wisdom as a blessing.

At every turn the people of Israel turned their backs on their Lord. They lied, killed, raped, stole, and disgraced the land that they stole with corruption. Yet the Lord continued to show them mercy.

More importantly, the Black People of Canaan were killed because of their alleged sinful ways, which caused the full wrath of the Lord to fall upon them. Yet the people of Israel did the same things and more, and their population was not annihilated liked the Black people. Which leads one to believe that the People of Ham had to have done something far worse than just worshipping another God for them to be hated so entirely.

While it is true the people of Ham worshipped a different God, their practices were not profane. Astarte, for example, was the Goddess of Love and Fertility. Asherah was another of the Fertility Goddesses. Yet the practices involved required a simple setting up of poles under green trees to pay homage. Far from burning children alive!

Likewise, Ashtoreth was a Syrian Goddess and Phoenician Goddess of sexual Love and Fertility, as was Dagon, who was Chief God of the Philistines and later the Phoenicians. Dagon was represented as half man, half fish. He was the Babylonian God of the Earth, while Ishtar was the Assyrian and Babylonian Goddess of Love and Fertility. Baal was identified as a mountain God. As a proper name it refers to a deity who is the master of the universe, but whom acquired such by military force. This is symbolic of the Lord.

As you will notice, there were only two separate manifestations of the deity: God and the Goddess. One viewed as the Master of the Universe, or Light, Truth, and Reason; and the other as the creative powers and forces of nature. All of the other deities were mere manifestations of these two principal concepts. The use of deities was to explain and demonstrate difficult philosophies and mystical truths.

The best example of this is with Egypt. The Greek historian Herodotus was informed by the Egyptian priests that no one could fully understand the teachings unless they first understood the dynasties of the gods and the pre-dynastic teachings. With careful instruction of the higher knowledge, the symbolic gods and goddesses were gradually worked into the teachings to illuminate the deeper knowledge of man and the possibilities open to him; namely, the possibility of become a living god.

The symbolic figures of the Egyptian gods were used solely to pass on knowledge to everyone sincere in mind, thereby feeding each person in accordance with his or her ability to comprehend.

"Menes", 1st Dynastic King of Egypt.

In pre-dynastic Egyptian teachings we encounter Temu, also referred to as Menes. He was the first man in pre-dynastic Egypt to have ascended and become a divine being in flesh. He was therefore referred to as a living god. In fact, interestingly, the Biblical Lord used this very term as a reference to Himself.

In hieroglyphics, Temu is depicted as a human being. He wears two crowns: one white, the other red. The scepter and ankh are his insignia. The crowns represent the north and north kingdoms of Egypt. Upper Egypt (extending to Ethiopia also called Nubia) was the southern kingdom and had the white crown. Lower Egypt (towards the Mediterranean Sea) was the northern kingdom, and had the red crown. After a war that was led by Temu against the northern kingdom, Temu conquered lower Egypt and united the land as one (circa 3200 B.C.). Temu wore the white crown over the red.

Since Temu developed his spiritual essence while on earth, the southern crown was worn atop the red crown. The white crown signified spiritual consciousness that was enlightened. Thus it is implied, the red crown signified the body and earthly self.

Temu was depicted as enlightened-minded. According to Temu's own instructions, enlightenment is best studied within. Maybe this is why on the Egyptian temples there were messages for the Black races that read, "Know thy self."

Correspondingly, this concept of enlightenment is very familiar. It is what the Buddhist and Hindus seek through meditation and fasting. Even the Muslim prophet Muhammad was first educated by a group called the Hunafa, who taught him to fast and mediate. This practice allowed him to become receptive, at which time during meditation he received the divine words from what was called the Messenger of God. It told him to read from his heart. At which time he revealed from within the divine text we know as the Holy Quran.

Every prophet regardless of their teachings and faith obtained spiritual consciousness and divine messages by practicing these basic tools. Christians also meditate, however they call this act prayer. Therefore all these concepts share the same basic philosophies, except in the ancient teachings. Having escaped the clutches of matter and liberated the spiritual essence called mind, such enlightenment led those who practiced to become living gods. Others perceive this as ensuring a place in Heaven once leaving the physical world.

However misunderstood, this is, in fact, also true. Hermes Trismegistus said all things vibrate. In other words, things of the spiritual aspect of yourself have frequencies. When you constantly think positively and do good things, you utilize the positive spiritual aspects of yourself. You begin to vibrate on a higher frequency. Like a magnet, your frequencies attract like frequencies into your surroundings. This is the source of good luck that people call the Blessings of God. Yet, when you constantly do evil things you begin to vibrate on a low frequency. This attracts negative into your surroundings – the source of all misfortune. The constant practice of negativity becomes a fixed frequency in your life, as does positivity. When your spiritual self leaves the body, whatever your final frequency is, will determine your place in the spiritual realm - the lower or the upper realms of spirituality.

Understanding this concept further explains these statements by Jesus Christ, "Things that come out of the mouth come from the heart. Those are the things that make you unclean. Evil thoughts come out of the heart, so do murder, adultery…stealing…and telling lies. Those are the things that make you unclean" (Matthew 15:18-20).

Also he said, "What I am about to tell you is true. What you lock on earth will be locked in heaven. What you unlock on earth will be unlocked in Heaven" (Matthew 18:18).

In the pre-dynastic teachings of Egypt we encounter concepts of self-reliance. Amen Ra was depicted as a son of God with the head of the hawk or falcon. The relationship to the sun relays that he is a self-reliant existence that gives life and light. This is also a symbol of truth and wisdom. Since Amen refers to the hidden, this implies that the self-reliant source of light and truth is hidden within.

The story of Osiris and Isis depicts a tale of resurrection and evolution of consciousness in it stellar, lunar, and solar phases. The idea of resurrection is an ancient and integral part of the African psyche. We are taught the powers of spiritual consciousness once enlightened can overcome death. For, while the body is matter and destructible, the sublime consciousness is not matter; and thus, cannot be destroyed because it is immortal.

This can also be realized in the Goddess Mut, who is the female counterpart of Amen Ra. She wears the vulture's cap and is depicted as the Phoenix. The creative forces of Mut burn her nest with fire and form the ashes rise the eternal bird. Thus, resurrection.

The complexity of the ideas could only be manifested in tales that would best be understood to children; in other words, anyone without understanding of his nature and the mysteries of the self in relation to God.

These concepts were told in great tales comprising a variety of persons and gods. But the reality is that this was a revelation of one god, and his many attributes in both the male and female aspects. Thus, derived a complex system that included various symbols. These symbols hold important keys for they too are used in the Biblical text. They had to use the ancient symbols for the wise understood the true meaning, while the profane were kept blind and subject to misinterpretations of their readings. In fact, several books in the Bible indicate that many portions of the Bible were concealed at the behest of the

Lord. Jesus Christ thus came to explain, but also spoke in the ancient symbols and parables. The purpose of this book is to explain without use of ancient symbols.

The Arcane Sciences

The Egyptian symbols, philosophies, as well as Astrology are critical to comprehending the basis of the Biblical text as well. In Genesis, on day four God created the lights in the sky, both lesser and greater to serve as signs to mark off the seasons, as well as give light on earth and separate light from darkness. This in essence not only covers Astronomy but Astrology as well.

The Chaldeans of Babylon, who were said to be Egyptian priests, only recognized seven planets. Correspondingly, Hermes Trismegistus also referred to seven spirits of the planets, also referred to as seven races or seven wheels and spheres. Likewise, the Bible refers to seven churches in Revelations, seven horns, etc. I wondered whether there was any connection. In order to analyze this I was required to understand the basis of Astrology.

Hermes Trismegistus stated that upon death the spiritual aspect of man must return the powers to the Seven Governors. He ascended the seven Rings returning to the Moon, the power to increase and diminish. The Egyptians associated the Moon with the Goddesses Hathor and Isis, both of whom were fertility Goddesses. The second ring was Mercury, which was returned an ability to devise, invent, design, and plot. Not just any plotting, but a crafty plot, scheme, or action usually intended to achieve an evil purpose. The Romans associated Mercury with Hermes, a messenger God to the other Gods. He was the God of Science and the protector of travelers, thieves, vagabonds, and commerce.

Mercury depicted with a staff of two snakes that wind around it. Gmünder Studien

The third Ring was Venus, which was returned the powers of lust and passions. The Romans called this Aphrodite, the Goddess of Love and Beauty.

The Sun received its powers of ambition. The Sun was a symbol of Ra by the Egyptians. The planet Mars then received the powers of rashness and boldness. This was the Roman God of War.

To Jupiter was given a sense of accumulations and riches. And to Saturn, which was the gate of Chaos, was returned falsehood and evil plotting.

Accordingly, Astrology teaches an ancient concept regarding the connection of the Cosmos to man. We are taught the effects of the Heavens upon man and are given clues to the origins of spirit.

In Astrology, the Universe above is seen as a greater manifestation of what occurs below. As Hermes Trismegistus informs us, "As above, so below." Based on seven planets, there was fashioned a Heavenly man or universal man, who is the perfect man. And in recognition of this perfect man, we are taught about our nature.

In this teaching, the Sun is viewed as the spirit. The Moon is viewed as the soul. The seven planets collectively made up the parts of the Heavenly man's body.

The head of the Heavenly man was the Sun. His feet were the crescent moon. To signify the circular oval shape of the Heavenly man, he was bent around where the soles of His feet touched against the back of his head. A symbol of this resulting manifestation can be seen in the Muslim flag.

Here a single star rests in the center of the crescent moon.

We also encounter a similar reference in Revelations 12:1 wherein a woman cloaked in the Sun was standing on the Moon and wore a crown of 12 stars.

To truly understand the relationship between the cosmic man and earthly man, we must first understand light, energy, and the consequent forces involved in solar, lunar, and stellar interactions. Therefore, I will provide a brief crash course.

Light is a small portion of what is termed the electromagnetic spectrum. All of the components of the electromagnetic spectrum are a series of vibrating electrical and magnetic fields travelling together in wavelengths. Each individual wave has its own frequency. These individual electromagnetic waves comprise the entire electromagnetic spectrum. They include from the lowest to the highest: microwaves, radio waves, infrared waves or cradiation visible light (which covers a small portion of the spectrum), ultraviolet radiation, x-rays, and gamma rays. Visible light travels on wavelengths with frequencies between 400_{NM} and 770_{NM}.

The eye recognizes light frequencies of different wavelengths as being different colors. The shorter waves (with high frequencies) are seen as blue. The longer waves (with low frequencies) are seen as the reds. Those frequencies with energies greater or lesser than physical light that we can see, are on the higher ends, ultraviolet; and, on the lower ends, infrared. They lay just outside of the visible spectrum.

White light is a mixture of visible light frequencies from all parts of the visible light spectrum. When these frequencies clash together they form white light, which tends to cancel each other out similar to loud static on a radio caused by interference in radio waves.

Celestial bodies that don't emit light (planets) are seen by the light they reflect or transmit (like the Moon). When these frequencies of the entire spectrum pass through a body, or when they are reflected off the surface of a celestial body, certain wavelengths may be absorbed. The body then displays the wavelengths that are rejected and reflected as a specific color. For example, grass would appear green because it absorbs all wavelengths except those associated with frequencies of green. These wavelengths are rejected and cannot even enter the body so they are reflected back, almost like bouncing off the surface of the body. When we look at the grass, we see it as green because this is the wavelength being thrown at us.

In this same fashion, Black bodies appear black because they reject no light frequencies. Instead, they absorb all of these cosmic energies. This makes a Black body a very harmonious and powerful body. Since no light is rejected, no light is coming back to the eye. Hence the bodies appear dark. A white body rejects all light. These wavelengths bounce off the bodies and clash, cancelling out their wavelengths. When you see the body, you see all these wavelengths of light being thrown back and clashing. Therefore, it appears white.

In science we learn that when electrical current is applied to an iron object it becomes a very powerful magnet. When the electrical current ceases, the iron object ceases to act like a magnet.

Correspondingly, all planets contain an iron core – some with great iron than others. The Sun and stars therefore act as providers of electrical currents, while the planets and Moon are transmitters of these solar and stellar frequencies. Once the planets become electrified with these cosmic energies they create a variation of universal forces that have causes and effects. These intensified vibratory energies are cast into our own magnetic atmosphere.

From the seven planets are transmitted seven primary colors or wavelengths, which Hermes Trismegistus states are the Seven Spirits of the planets, the Seven Governors, Seven Races, Wheels, and Rings. We know from Hermes Trismegistus the powers they give, but the intensity of these powers at any given time depends upon the constant changes in the positions of the Sun, start and planets in relation to the Earth as it travels in its elliptical orbit around the Sun. There are four major points on the orbit around the Sun, which are similar to the 12, 3, 6, and 9 positions on a clock. The space between these four points contains 12 stations all together. The four points are the four seasons. Between one point to the next, you encounter three phases of the season. These are astrological signs. This is why each season contains approximately three months, each with its own sign.

These signs are based upon what planets and stars are closest, and the vibrating magnetic field's intensity as the planets transmit these vibratory energies into our atmosphere.

When a child is born and his umbilical cord is cut, the child's first breath on his own inhales the electrically charged atmosphere and these electrically charged atoms in the air are absorbed into the lungs and heart. At that very moment the child's body begins to vibrate at the distinct frequency of the atmosphere. The child's frequency becomes fixed at that moment and will remain traveling in that distinct frequency throughout his or her life. This moment is then called their sign. The wavelength may fluctuate depending upon the child or person's thinking.

The person's distinct frequency also adopts a color. This is also termed one's Aura, which is visible to clairvoyants. This becomes a person's immediate magnetic field surrounding his or her body. People have five points of projection from which streams vital forces or energies. These points are said to be the head, hands, and feet represented by the symbol of the five-point star or pentagram, which is also referred to as a pentacle.

Yet later on the Israelites adopted the six-pointed Star of David, which adds the penis as a sixth point of projection. The Pentacle is thus the female, while the hexagram is the male.

Mason's all-seeing eye or Eye of Horus, the Star of David, and Pentacle.

These radiated energies from the points of projection correspond to the seven rays of forces that relate to the seven creative forces of nature; in other words, the seven rays or colors of the seven planets. Each zone has its own powers and is determined to be pure or impure based on levels of brightness or dullness. Recall that Hermes Trismegistus stated these powers destroy in lower man, and give life in Heavenly man. Similarly, lower desires dull your sphere, while the exercise of spiritual abilities illuminate it.

If you are a person who constantly does evil, you have evil thoughts. This causes your head to project low or dull frequencies. When you live your life under a dull frequency, in death, your spirit will be trapped in this low frequency upon release form the body. And to these low frequencies is where you will return, to a lower place some refer to as Hell. Those who are liberated in brightness and high frequencies will travel to higher frequencies. Some call this Heaven. This is why the Bible teaches us to refrain from evil thinking and overindulgence of lower desires.

While living, your low and dull frequencies also attract those frequencies into your midst. This is the source of bad luck. If you are one with a bright and high frequency, you are going to attract these bright frequencies to you. This becomes the source of good luck.

Under the Zodiac signs there are powerful talismans for each sign, which are also called birthstones. They are said to attract the frequencies needed for that sign and enhance one's productivity and success in thought. Your thinking will resonate on a positive and productive frequency. This is seen in the Bible. If you examine the Book of Exodus 28:15-21, the Lord instructs Moses to make a chest cloth that contains the twelve gemstones of the Zodiac. It reads, "Make a chest cloth that will be used for making decisions…"

The twelve astrological signs are listed in order below, along with their specific birthstone, corresponding element, and both Egyptian significance and Biblical relationship to the twelve tribes of Israel.

Aries: The highest of the fire trinity element. Its constellation is Mars. Its symbol is the Ram. In Egypt the God Amen/Ammon was represented with the ram's head. He was the God of Life and Reproduction. Aries is symbolic to sacrifice. This sign represents the head and brains of the Heavenly man. The birthstones are Amethyst and diamond.

Taurus: The highest of the Earth element trinity. Its birthstone is the sapphire. The ruling planet is Venus. Its symbol is the bull. In Egyptian philosophy it was the sacred bull called Apis. Taurus is symbolic of the procreative forces in nature. It governs the lymphatic system, and is associated with the ears, neck, and throat of the Heavenly man.

Gemini: First of the airy element trinity. Its planet is Mercury, gemstone is the emerald, and it symbolizes unity and strength. The sign represents the hands and arms of the Heavenly man. On the esoteric level, it relates to the tribes of Simeon and Levi in the Bible.

Cancer: Highest of the watery element trinity. Its gem is the pearl and Moonstone; constellation is the Moon; and its symbol is the crab, a symbol of tenacity. It represents the vital organs of the Heavenly man.

Leo: Second fiery trinity element. Its constellation is the Sun and gemstone is the ruby. On an esoteric plane it refers to the Biblical Judah. The sign reveals the ancient mysteries of sacrifice and compensations. It represents the heart of the Heavenly man.

Virgo: Second of the Earthly trinity element. Its planet is mercury and gemstone is sard onyx. It signifies the solar plexus of the Heavenly man. On an esoteric plane it refers to the Biblical tribe of Asher.

Libra: Second airy trinity element. Its constellation is Venus and gemstone is Chrysolite. Libra symbolizes justice and represents the loins of Heavenly man. On an esoteric plane it refers to the Biblical tribe of Dan.

Scorpio: Second of the water element trinity. Scorpio's constellation is Mars and gemstone is topaz. In the symbolic aspect, it represents death and deceit. It is called the allegorical serpent of matter, causing the fall of man from Libra (the point of equilibrium) to degradation and death by deceit of Scorpio. It is the emblem of the generation of life. It represents the procreative attributes of the Heavenly man, and is concerned with the ancient mysteries of the ancient phallic rites and secrets of sex. On an esoteric plane it refers to the Biblical tribe of Gad.

Sagittarius: The lowest of the fiery element trinity. The planet is Jupiter and gemstone is turquoise. The symbol is the centaur, a symbol of authority and wordly wisdom. It represents the thighs and muscular foundation of the Heavenly man.

Capricorn: The lowest of the Earthly trinity. The planet is Saturn and gemstone is onyx. Capricorn, in its symbolic aspect, represents sin. It represents the knees of the Heavenly man. Upon the esoteric plane it corresponds to the Biblical tribe of Naphatali.

Aquarius: Last of the airy trinity element. The gemstone is garnet and ruling planet is Uranus. Aquarius symbolizes judgment and corresponds to the legs of the Heavenly man. It is the water bearer on the esoteric plane, and refers to the Biblical tribe of Reuben.

Pisces: The last of the element water trinity. Its planet is Neptune and gemstone is the bloodstone. It signifies the feet of the Heavenly man, and symbolizes the flood and baptism by water. It is the emblem of obedience.

The *Harmonia Macrocosmica* of Andreas Cellarius

In this philosophy, the seven planets were divided. The Sun represented the Spirit, the Moon represented the Soul, and the remaining five planets represented the senses. The Chaldeans created fables and allegories to teach these principles to their youth.

The ancient application of the Zodiac philosophies also caused the creation of a hidden language known only to those taught the Mysteries. For example, each sign had a meaning and was also associated with a body part on the Heavenly man. This became an ancient sign language by which the adepts were able to communicate with one another. Aries means, "I am." Taurus, "I have." Gemini, "I think." Cancer, "I feel." Leo, "I will." Virgo, "I analyze." Libra, "I balance." Scorpio, "I desire." Sagittarius, "I see." Capricorn, "I use." Aquarius, "I know." And Pisces, "I believe."

Further, the right ear represented understanding and hearing. The right eye referred to identify. The mouth referred to conceptualization. The right nostril referred to respond. The left nostril referred to sense. The left ear referred to view point. The left eye referred to energetic. The head to "I am able." The throat to "have." The lungs, head, chest, and forehead to "think." The stomach to "feel." The heart to will. The full hand to personality. The abdominal to "analyze." The kidneys to balance. Genitals referred to desire. Hips and thighs to "I see." Knees to "I use." Calves and ankles to "I know." Feet to believe. Thumb to relate. Index finger to "I create." Second finger to personality. Ring finger to being. And pinky to manifest.

An advanced form of this communication is used by Masons to this very day to identify one another and communicate ideas to each other. Thus, this is done practically in front of people who have not been initiated and yet the people look but don't see. They are rendered blind.

The symbols of antiquity such as the pyramids, Ankh, Sphinx, Obelisk, etc. all have hidden meanings. They were signs to the Black race for all time, but that knowledge was stolen. When that occurred, the Blacks became lost and lacked the ability to find their way back to the state that made them the first civilization of the world.

The Masons were trained in these mysteries by the Egyptians. These ancient symbols of Masonry are seen illustrated in the Biblical text as well. Yet we tend to overlook them because we were not educated in the mysteries of the ancient civilizations. Let me demonstrate a few of these Masonic instruments then offer you their meanings.

In the Book of Amos 7:7-8, we read the third version of Amos in which he sees the Lord standing by a wall built very straight. The Lord was holding a plum line. The Lords ask Amos, "What do you see?" Amos replies, "A plumb line." The Lord replies, "Look at what I am doing. I am hanging a plumb line next to my people to show how crooked they are."

In the Book of Zechariah 2:1-2, it states, "Then I looked up and saw a man. He was holding a measuring line. 'Where are you going?' I asked. 'To measure Jerusalem,' he answered. 'I want to find how wide and how long it is.'"

In the Book of Job 38:4-6, the Lord speaking to Job asks, "Where were you when I laid the Earth's foundations? Tell me if you know. Who measured it? I am sure you know! Who stretched measuring line across it? What was it built on? Who laid its most important stone?..."

The Arcane meaning of the tools of Masonry are as follows:
1. The Square: The square is used to measure our lives and to make the corners of our conduct square. Symbolically, it represents the material and physical self. The lower self is ruled by the Laws of Nature, made manifest in the square. The circle is symbolic of the spiritual self, which is governed by the Laws of Heaven. The square resides within the confines of the circle. The dumb, deaf, and blind see the circle as existing within the confines of the square. To them, they are subjected to death because they believe in death.
2. The Compass: The compass circumscribes circles around our passions and desire to keep them within the boundaries of spiritual righteousness.
3. The Mallet and the Chisel: The mallet and chisel are used by the skilled worker to cut away all the knotty and rough edges of unrighteousness. It makes the board or stone fit the builder's useful purpose.
4. The Plumb Line: The plumb line is used by the skilled worker to test uprightheousness. It reveals whether a person's conduct is upright or crooked.
5. The Level: The level is used by the skilled worked to mark the manner of equality and fair or just dealings. It exposes whether our actions are fair and just.
6. The Trowel: The trowel is used by the skilled worker to evenly spread the cement mixture, which is comprised of love, peach, truth, freedom, wisdom, and justice. This very cement is what unites all into the mystic ties of brotherhood.
7. The 12-step Ladder: The ladder is used by the skilled worker to ascend to the Temple of the Perfected Man, the pinnacle of that which we spend our life to build. The temple is the body, built with indestructible materials. Thus it is called the stone. The stone body is built to house

the awakened and sublime being within. These 12 steps can be understood as the 12 Zodiac signs and the mystical powers they possess when applied to the self.

8. The 24 Inch Gauge: The gauge divides time into three parts. Eight hours for rest, work, and family.
9. The Gavel or Maul: This tool is used by the skilled worker to fit the stones with order, and ensure they are firmly set in place. It thus secures the foundation of the temple and was used in the construction of the Heavens and Earth.

Understanding these symbolic and arcane meanings allows you to become a skilled worker, able to build yourselves and others into perfect stones and to ascend in life to reach that place of spirituality that brings peace and harmony as well as success in your undertakings.

These concepts were derived from Egyptian mysteries but were reapplied under Masonry because of the persecutions of the Church to those who dealt with Arcane Sciences. However the Black race were not Masons. Masons were the students who were taught by Cain and became travelling men in his likeness, wandering the Earth. Most of whom were people of Seth.

Application of Arcane Sciences

When we look at how the Black giants were slaughtered, we discover that the special manner in which they were killed included beheading, and cutting off their big toes, thumbs, and earlobes. I immediately wondered whether this was because some of the giants were said to have had six toes and fingers, as noted in 2 Samuel 21:20. Yet, this was quickly ruled out.

This could not have been the cause of the secret ritualistic killings because in the book of Judges 1:6-7 we read about Israel's attack on king Adoni-Bezek, wherein it states, " ...They cut off his thumbs and big toes. Then Adoni-Bezek proclaimed, 'I cut off the thumbs and big toes of 70 kings. I made them pick up scraps at my table. Now the Lord has paid me back for what I did to them.'"

Here we find an interesting clue that indicates this was payback! This payback became a mark on Israel, a ritual taught to the people of Levi who served as the high priests after they had left Egypt.

The Bible illustrates that the priests were prepared and anointed as priests of the Lord by slaughtering a ram. The very same symbol of Aries, and the symbol that represented Amen/Ammon, the God of Life. The ram's blood was placed on the priest's right ear lobe, on his right thumb, and on the big toes of their feet (Exodus 29:19-20; Leviticus 8:23-24). This was not a coincidence! To serve the Lord as a priest required them to first be of the tribe of Levi, which was represented by the sign Gemini. They were inducted into priesthood by this ritual, illustrating opposition to the God of Life. They were also taught by this ritual to forever remember picking scraps at the tables of the Black race. They were to remember being servants while the Blacks were masters. This was also symbolized by the construction of the sacred linen apron (Exodus 28: 6-13).

As you may recall the apron was made by 'skilled workers' only, and contained two onyx stones with six names on each stone. These names were the twelve tribes of Israel listed in the order of their births to coincide with each sign of the Zodiac.

Freemasons are also familiar with this linen apron as it was worn by them during ceremonial initiations into the Mysteries. In the Bible all priests wore this apron (1 Samuel 22:18) as well as the first King Samuel (1 Samuel 2:18) and King David (1 Samuel 21:9; 23:9; 30:7; 2 Samuel 6:14).

When Adoni-Bezek referred to 70 kings he was referring to the 70 elders of Israel who accompanied Moses, Araaon, Nadab, and Abihu up Mount Sinai where they saw God (Exodus 24:1-11). These people of Israel were strangers and outsiders in the Black land and had not been readily accepted into the mysteries of the Ancients. The Black race were not outsiders, and of them Eliphaz states to Job, "I'll tell you what those who are wise have said. They don't hide anything they've received from their people of long ago. The land was given only to those people. Their wisdom did not come from outsiders" (job 15:18-19). In contrast, the people of Seth were considered outsiders both in the land of Canaan (Exodus 6:4), as well as in Egypt (Exodus 22:21). Thus their wisdom was received like scraps from the master's table, not from their own people.

This is verified in the New Testament Book of Mark 7:25-2 wherein a Greek women came to Jesus and asked for his help. Therein Jesus says, "First let the children eat all they want. It is not right to take the children's bread and throw it to their dogs. The woman of Seth then replied, 'Yes Lord but even the dogs under the table eat the children's crumbs." Jesus then replied, "That was a good reply."

This exchange was symbolic. The children referenced the Black people. The bread referred to food of thought; thus, knowledge, wisdom, and understanding. The crumbs refer to small portions of the wisdom and the dogs refer to the people of Seth. We know this was not literal food based on Jesus' statement "I am the bread of life. No one who comes to me will ever go hungry" (John 6:35). This was clearly a reference to wisdom. Therefore we know the analogy of the table and the scraps of food were symbolic references to wisdom, of which only small bits and pieces were obtained, like scraps by the outsiders.

"Think about this," Jesus told his disciples in Matthew 13:11-12, "You have been given the chance to understand the secrets of the Kingdom of Heaven. It has not been given to outsiders." And Jesus knew this for he himself was educated in Egypt as a child (Matthew 2:13-14).

In the book of Hosea the Lord spoke about Israel and stated, "Now it is said about them. You are not my people but at that time they will be called children of the living God" (Hosea 1:10). Also, Israel will be called Jezreel. That is because I will answer her prayers. I will plant her in the land for myself. I will show my love to the one I called not my loved one. I will say you are my people to those who were called not my " (Hosea 2:22-23).

It is evident from these Biblical passages that the people of Seth were outsiders. It is also evident that a secret plot was transpiring in which the old world order was to be supplanted by a new world order. This plot led to genocide, and the theft of the Black races' land as well as the destruction of their culture.

The people of Israel were involved in a conspiracy to destroy the Black culture as well as the truth about their origins. For the Earth was given to the original people not the outsiders. The original Black bodies which were in harmony with the Universe and contained all the vibrant energies that permeate the atmosphere. To them, was all ancient wisdom given. This is why Jesus stated about Ethiopia in the book of Matthew 12:42, "The Queen of the South will stand up on judgment day with the people now living. And she will prove that they are guilty! She came from far away to listen to Solomon's wisdom.

We know the Queen of the South refers to Ethiopia because the queen of Sheba was the queen that came from Ethiopia to test king Solomon, as shown in 1 Kings 10:1-13.

Thus, Jesus bears witness that the original people will stand up among those now claiming to be wise and fathers of the ancient mysteries and will prove that they are guilty of murder and theft, as well as lies, and enslavement of the true masters of the Kingdom of Heaven, while concealing from those rightful descendants the truth of their ancestors and the knowledge they are the sons of God and the giants of long ago.

While the people of Seth were exposed to the great wisdom of the Black race they did not understand these great mysteries. Having only received scraps, this is why they burned their children alive; yet, those chosen few who were taught became the masons of old time. This is evidenced in the Bible.

Abraham was educated by the high priest Melchizideck and also went into Egypt to live for a while. He was treated well and had dwelled in the palace of the Pharaoh and was thus, introduced to the Mysteries (Genesis 12:10).

Lets review Genesis for a second, wherein the Lord appears to Abraham near the large mamre trees. Mamre was the Lord of the area and an Amorite (Genesis 14:13). He and his two brothers had previously aided Abraham in battle (Genesis 14:24). Now as Abraham sits near the trees of mamre he sees three men standing nearby. He quickly leaves his tent and bows low, saying, "My Lord if you are pleased with me don't pass me by." He offers the travelers food and water for their strength (Genesis 18:1-8).

After these three men ate, drank, and washed up they departed. The question here is how did Abraham know this was the Lord? They obviously appeared in human form so how did Abraham know. First, it is because Masons have a sign language that is known to one another. Abraham most likely learned this while in Egypt or from Melchizedeck. This reference to the Lord appearing as a man needing to rest and eat also reveals a hidden truth about the Lord. The Lord was man. Which is why he refers to himself as the living God. Because he was alive! In flesh and was seen as a master mason.

In Genesis chapter 19 these same three individuals traveled to Sodom, two of which actually entered Sodom. When Lot sees these two people he bows down to them and says, "My Lords, please come to my house you can wash your feet and spend the night there. Then you can go on your way early in the morning" (Genesis 19:1-2).

Here Lot also recognizes the men for who they really are, which shows Lot also was skilled in this secret communication. His statement also illustrates there was more than one Lord. But how can there have been more than one Lord you may ask. Recall that Lord is defined primarily as a man who is a master in a given field or activity. Masons who master their degrees and teachings fit this definition. We know that these were people because when the men of Sodom saw them they surrounded Lot's home wanting to have sex with them (19: 5). We also see that the people of Sodom had no idea who they were dealing with, an indication that these people were not trained in the Mysteries.

Correspondingly we encounter Jacob becoming a master mason in Genesis 28: 0-22, wherein it states, "Jacob reached a certain place and stopped for the night. The sun had set. He took one of the stones there and placed it under his head. Then he lay down to sleep. In a dream he saw a stairway standing on Earth, the top reached the Heavens. The Angels of God were going up and coming down on it. The Lord stood above the stairway. He said I am the Lord. I am the God of your grandfather Abraham and the God of Isaac. I will give you and the children after you the land on which you are lying. I am with you. I will watch over you where you go. And will bring you back to this land. I will not leave you until I have done what I promised you. When Jacob woke up from his sleep he thought, the Lord is certainly in this place and I didn't even know it. Jacob became afraid and said how holy is this place. This must be the house of God this is the gate of heaven! When morning came, Jacob took the stone he had placed under his head. He set it up as a pillar and poured oil on it. He named the place Bethel but the city used to be called Luz. Then Jacob made a promise. He said, "Then you Lord will be my God. This stone I've set up as a pillar will be God's house and I'll give you a tenth of everything you give me. This stone mentioned here was not a rock. Nobody places their head on a rock as if it were a pillow to sleep. It would be very uncomfortable. But the Bible tells us what the meaning of a stone is. In Revelations 2:17, it mentions a letter written to the church in Pergamum. The letter reads, "Those who have ears should listen. I will give hidden food to those who overcome. I will also give each of them a white stone with a new name written on it. Only the one who receives the name will know what it is."

Correspondingly, in 1 Peter 2:4-8 it reads, "Christ is the living stone. You are also living stones. As you come to him you are being built into a house for worship. In scripture, it says look I am placing a stone in Zion. It is a chosen and very valuable stone. It is the most important stone in the building the one who trusts in him will never be put to shame. The stone is very important to you who believe. But to people who do not believe, the stone the builders did not accept has become the most important stone of all. And it is a stone that causes people to trip. It is a rock that makes them fall. They trip and fall because they do not obey the message. That is also what God planned for them.

Here we are taught the stone is a person. Thus a person was placed in Zion the one who trusted in him would not be put to shame. Recall shame deals with the absence of clothes as in the case of Noah. Thus, the stones were people but a person who was well skilled in the Mysteries. These people are possessors of the ancient wisdom as is revealed in the temptation of Jesus. For example, in Matthew 4:1-4, the devil tempted Jesus saying, "If you are the Son of God tell the stones to become bread. Jesus replied, 'It is written man doesn't live on bread alone. He also lives on every word of God.' This indicates that he recognized the stones as wise individuals for he would not change the wisdom for mere physical food.

So when we read that Jacob placed a stone under his head and from it had received a message we are being informed of a lodge where masons are taught and initiated. We know that this stone was in a city because Jacob had called it Bethel (previously called Luz). We also see that Jacob set it up as a pillar, which is defined in this context as a place that occupies a central or responsible position very similar to the function of the lodge. Lastly, recall the words of Jacob, "This must be the house of God."

We further know this was a not merely a rock but associated with a place, a lodge based on Isaiah 51:1. "…Listen to me you who do what is right. Pay attention, you who look to me. Consider the rock you were cut out of. Think about the rock pit you were dug from."

Thus we learn that Jacob, too, was initiated into the mysteries.

Ishmael who was half Black received a wife from Egypt (Genesis 21:21). Thus, he was also exposed to the ancient philosophies of Egypt through his wife and mother; which may account for why his descendants, the Midianites, were claimed to worship the sun, Moon, and stars.

Again we see Jacob's education into the mysteries at fruitation. In Genesis 32: 22-31 it recounts Jacob's confrontation with God, stating that Jacob was left alone. "A man struggled with him until morning. The man saw that he couldn't win. So he touched the inside of Jacob's hip. As Jacob struggled with the man Jacob's hip was twisted. Then the man said, 'Let me go. It is morning.' But Jacob replied 'I won't let you go unless you bless me.' The man asked him, 'What is your name?' 'Jacob,' he answered. Then the man said, 'your name will be Israel for you have struggled with God and with man and you have won.'" So Jacob named the place Peniel. He said, "I saw God face to face but I am still alive."

There are some factors that should leap out to you. First, the man here did not know Jacob's name, which is interesting for the god not to recognize the same person he previously blessed. Also, Jacob asks for a blessing. This indicates the person who was the lord was not the person who was god here.

To understand the riddle of the hip, let's return to the Zodiac's secret language. The hip is a body part associated with the sign Sagittarius and it means, "I see."

Therefore, in a struggle under the cloak of darkness Jacob struggled with his lower self until the sun began to rise. The rising of the sun shows a period of spiritual enlightenment, the light beginning to dawn on him and overcome his darkness. When the light came forth, Jacob's hip was touched. Thus, when the light came forth, Jacob began to SEE. A period of spiritual awakening occurred and he proclaimed, "I saw God!" Notice he did not proclaim to have seen the Lord. This was the point that Jacob became a master mason.

Therefore, you can very clearly see the application of the secret sciences displayed throughout the Biblical passages. And it indicates that the outsiders were trained in the ancient wisdom, and yet had been conspiring for centuries to destroy the Black race.

As we continue, we see that Joseph also went to Egypt and presided in the royal palace (Genesis 41:39-41). In Egypt Joseph was given the name Zaphenath Paneah, and married an Egyptian priest's daughter. Thus it is evident, that as the son in law of an Egyptian priest, Joseph was taught the Egyptian mysteries and philosophies.

According to the historian Diodorus Herodotus, in the second clement of Alexandria there were six orders of Egyptian priests and each order was mathematically mastered to coincide with the 42 books of Hermes. Clement described a procession of the Egyptian priests calling them by their orders, and stating their qualifications as follows: First, was the singer Odus bearing an instrument of music. He is required to know by heart two of the books of Hermes; one containing the hymns of the Gods, and the other, the allotment of the king's life. Next, was Horoscopus carrying in his hands a sundial (compass) and a palm branch, the symbols of astronomy. He must master by heart four books of Hermes dealing with astronomy. Next, is the hierogrammat with feathers on his head, a book in his hand, and a rectangle (a rectangular case with writing materials such as the writing ink and the reed). He has to know the hieroglyphics, cosmography, geography, astronomy, the topography of Egypt, the sacred utensils and measures, the temple's furniture, and the lands. He also must know the books of Hermes regarding the slaughter of animals. The Prophetess is the president of the temple and is required to know by heart the 10 books of Hermes, which contains the laws and doctrines concerning the Gods (secret theology) and the education of the priests.

The clement Herodotus makes clear that Egyptians forbid the writing down of any learning by the initiates. Herodotus was a student and had been initiated in the science of the monuments: pyramids, temples, libraries, obelisk, sphinx, idols, as well as in architecture, masonry, cemetery, engineering, sculpturing, metallurgy, agriculture, mining, and forestry.

The universe of Ptolemy is a diagrammatic representation of the relationships existing between the various divine & elemental parts of every creature. Three zodiac circles surround the planet's orbits, which are the Governors of the World. The four elemental spheres in the center represent the physical constitution of both man and the universe. From an old print, courtesy of Carl Oscar Borg

Finally we meet Moses who was raised in the Pharaoh's household from childbirth and taught the philosophies and mysteries of the Temple. He would later take these Egyptian teachings of the Temples, sacrifices of animals, the secrets of the sacred utensils, measures and furniture, and teach these to the people of Seth. These were revealed to them in books such as Exodus and Leviticus, resulting in the transfer of important mysteries concerning the Egyptians temples and practices from the Black race to the people of Seth.

The Origin Of The People Of Seth

In order to expose the origins of the people of Seth and the great secret that caused them to attack the Black race with such violence, we must first begin with Moses. For Moses is the final key to the entire puzzle. We previously discussed that Moses was educated in Egypt along with the royal household (Exodus 2:10). As a prince of Egypt, Moses was privileged to a very fine education. And while the Bible gives no mention as to how Moses grew up and where he went to school, we know that Moses being raised by the pharaoh's sister would have been given an Egyptian name and education.

The Egyptians had titled two of their cities Annu, wherein Ra was considered the most important deity. The best educated received their education therein. The fragments of Manetho indicates that Moses Egyptian name was Osarseph. He was a native of Annu, the northern Annu (Heliopolis). There he learned the secrets of the Egyptian teachings by his preceptors and the knowledge of One God was revealed to him along with all the symbols and devices. He was also, and most importantly, taught of a people whom were created by man approximately two thousand years before he was born.

As noted in Paul Guthie's making of the white man, the ancient Egyptians recorded the Tamahu, which is translated "created white people." The ancient Egyptian's writings refer to all whites as Typhonians, or the people of Seth.

Both the Biblical text and lost and found Muslim lessons of the Nation of Gods and Earths, indicate that Moses arrived approximately 2000 B.C. And two thousand years before him were a race of people whom were exiled. As well, approximately 600 years before such exile, this group was created by Yacub as a special people to rule over the original people.

Correspondingly, the word Falasha is a term used for the Black Jews living in Ethiopia. That Ethiopian word means exiled people or stranger.

The implications of this created people were too much for me to resist, so I wondered whether some trace of this would be evident in the Bible. And so I began to count backwards from Moses approximately 2600 years looking for a group called the people of Seth. I also wanted to see if there were any significant changes that occurred when they arrived.

When we add the entire period from the time Abraham was born until Moses, we encounter approximately 567 years. From the point of the ending of the flood to the point of Abraham's birth is approximately 292 years. Since Shem was 98 at such point, we add another 98 years and to arrive at the point Shem was born. This is now approximately 950 years before Moses was born. We are now at Noah, who was 500 years old.

When we continue backwards from Noah to Mahalel who was 65 when Jared was born (Genesis 5:15), we have traveled backwards approximately 2,043 years. Therefore around this period of time the people of Seth should have been in exile. European writers including Pliny have recorded that walls were built from one sea to another trapping the people of Seth in Europe.

As I continued searching for some clue of a people of Seth I traveled backwards from Mahalel to his great grandfather Seth! This brings me to about 2,400 years (Genesis 5:6-15), which is roughly an exact calculation of 2,600 years before Moses arrived. And sure enough I found the people of Seth.

So in this time I search for some significant changes in culture based on their arrival and find it at Genesis 5:1-3 which states, "When God created man he made him in his <u>own</u> likeness. He created them as male and female. He blessed them. But when Adam was 130 years old he had a son in his <u>own</u> likeness. He named him Seth."

You see, while God created man in his own image and likeness, these were the original people. But God did not make Seth. The passage reads, "Adam had a son in his own likeness. Seth was not in the likeness of God as were the original people, but rather in the likeness of man. Not man, but a likeness and replica of the original."

It was from Seth that people began to worship the Lord (Genesis 4:26). Prior to this time the original people had not worshipped at all.

This indicates that the concept of a chosen people and special people first was arrived here. The Nation of Gods and Earth indicate that Yacub had taught these people of Seth that they were special and that they would rule over the Black race. This is also evident because the concept of a chosen people for the Lord in regards to the Israelites is echoed throughout the Biblical text, as well as the conspiracy to destroy the Black race and take their lands as their own.

Moses, having been exposed to the truth about God and the secrets of the people of Seth, set out to raise his people up into a mighty nation in keeping with the idea first brought forth so long ago, that these were a chosen race to rule over the earth. He then united the people under the faith in the Demiurges – The Lord, the Demiurges, to whom the people of Seth had began to worship over two thousand years prior to his birth.

Clearly, this is why it is written that the Lord told Moses, "I want you to bring the Israelites out of Egypt. They are 'my' people" (Exodus 3:10).

In addition, he said, "Tell the Israelites the Lord is the Lord of your fathers…he has sent me to you" (Exodus 3:15). The Lord did not say that he was the god of the original people. Why? Because long ago, the original man had risen and become like one of the gods. Thus, he was not subservient to either man nor beast, for he was the alpha and the omega – the first and the last – and had entered the circle of life through the eye of the sun to replenish the Earth of all sin. Alpha is the divine man before descent into matter and omega is the symbol of the perfected man who regains perfection by passing through the cycle of life and resurrection in regards to his spiritual consciousness.

Moses too had passed through the circle of resurrection and was thus very aware of the originals man's divine nature. Moses was further instructed by the Lord in his arcane studies. The Lord taught and instructed Moses what to say when he encountered the pharaoh (Exodus 4:12). This increased Moses' knowledge and made him appear as if he was a god in the eyes of the pharaoh (Exodus 7:1). Moses was taught for over 50 years and had not been capable of approaching the pharaoh until he was approximately 80 years old (Exodus 7:7).

In Exodus 3:13-14, Moses asks the Lord what should he tell the people their God's name is. At which point the Lord says tell them, "I am has sent you."

Therefore, when the Israelites asked who God was, it was incumbent upon Moses to reply, "I am."

There is much speculation about the mistreatment of the Israelites in Egypt. This speculation is utilized to justify the slaughter that occurred. However the biblical text offers a slightly different version. This will clearly demonstrate that Moses did not take the Israelites out of Egypt because they were poorly treated, but rather because he learned the secret origins of the people of Seth.

Let's recall Joseph, who was sold into slavery by his own brothers, was also taken into the pharaoh's royal household. The pharaoh later gave the relatives of Joseph the best lands in Egypt (Genesis 47:11). The Israelites did not pay any taxes on the lands and were allowed to live peacefully. However, the Israelites began to overpopulate the land of Egypt (Exodus 1: 7). Now two major problems arise from overpopulation. First, the overpopulation of Egypt by a foreign group not obedient to the culture and laws would allow the Israelites to become the majority and the natives, minorities; which threatens the security of the government. Second, there is a distinct issue with space. In China, when the people became overpopulated, the government decreed that there would be a limit on the amount of children a couple could have. In fact, this is the very same concept that the pharaoh put into effect.

The pharaoh no longer allowed free room and board for the Israelites; instead, he put them to work. It was a mild idea that with work the Israelites would stop having as many children. But this failed to work and the number of children continued to increase (Exodus 1:12). At this point, the pharaoh ordered the nursemaids to allow the female babies to live, but not the males. This is because in the Israelite culture the family line was continued through the male.

However, despite this law, the Israelites continued their disobedience to the laws of a nation they resided in. So the pharaoh was left with no option but to order that all male babies be killed. This was the final result of least drastic measures.

Let us also recall that after the Israelites left Egypt they longed to go back. They reminisced saying to one another, "Remember the fish we ate in Egypt. It didn't cost us anything. We also remember the cucumbers, melons, leeks, onions, and garlic" (11:5). They also said, "We were better off in Egypt" (11:18).

This is a far cry from a mistreated people who were happy to be liberated from bondage.

Therefore the cause of Moses taking the people of Seth out of Egypt was not due to mistreatment but to teach them the sciences that he himself was taught in Egypt.

Moses was born to a Hebrew mother from the tribe of Levi (Exodus 2:1). The tribe of Levi came from Jacob and Leah (Genesis 35: 23). Leah had blue eyes and was the daughter of Laban (Genesis 29:16-17). Laban was an Aramean (Genesis 25:20); the root word of which is Aramj, and Aram is a descendant of Shem (Genesis 10:22). Thus, there is no question of the mixed genealogy of Moses.

Based on Moses ties with Levi he was inclined to participate in conspiracies. The tribe of Levi was well known for their secret plots and conspiracies. (Genesis 49:5-6). Thus the tribe of Levi was a group that was use to secrets and plotting, the likes of which we see in the fall of Canaan. Even the Jews today have a sect that believes Moses hid secret truths in the Biblical Torah. They call this the cabala or cabbala. Which is defined as an occult theosophy of rabbinical origins widely transmitted in medieval Europe based on secret interpretations of the Hebrew Scriptures. Also notice that the root word of cabala is cabal. Cabal is defined as a conspiratorial group of plotters or a secret scheme or plot.

The plot is not hard to comprehend. Moses informed the people of Israel, "The Lord will bring you into the land of the Canaanites, Hittites, Amorites, Hivittes, and Jebusites. He took an oath and promised your people of long ago that he would give that land to you" (Exodus 13:5). Of course this oath was unbeknownst to the Black race who would surely have put an end to the plot long before Abraham had children. Let us also pay attention to the term 'the Lord took an oath.' Oath is defined as a solemn declaration or promise to fulfill a pledge often calling upon God as a witness. This statement by definition implies that the Lord swore before a God other than himself. Which further illustrates that the Lord referred to, is distinct from God Most High.

According to Moses' own statements, he was a critical part of the plot. His bloodline connection also makes him more inclined to such schemes. If it quacks like a duck, it's a duck.

The plot was to target a selected group: Blacks. To rob and steal their land and cultural identity, as well as to annihilate and enslave them.

We know that this conspiracy had been growing steadily before Moses was born, based on the actions of some of these people of Seth in regards to Blacks.

Terah was the father of Abram, Nahor, and Haran (Genesis 11:26). Haran's daughter was Micah (Genesis 11:29), Micah married Nahor, her own uncle, and together they had a daughter called Rebekah (Genesis 24:15) Abraham's son, Isaac, married Rebekah (Genesis 25:20), who was his first cousin. Haran was also the father of Lot (Genesis 11:27). Lot slept with both his daughters and had children by them (Genesis 19:30-38). Amram, Levi's grandson (Exodus 6:16-18), slept with his own aunt, Jochebed (Exodus 6:20), and from that union came Moses and Araon.

Now the people of Seth did not have to practice incest. They chose to do so under a concept that they were special because they were created not in the image of God but in the likeness of man. So they practiced inbreeding to preserve their special genetics. A concept we see still carried own by the Aryan race.

In addition, the people of Seth frowned upon marriage with the Black race. When Abraham had a child by the Black Egyptian Hagar, his Sethonian wife, Sarah, had both Hagar and Ishmael exiled into the wilderness because Ishmael had laughed at his brother Isaac (Genesis 21: 8-11). Also, Abraham didn't want his son Isaac to have a Black wife, so Isaac married Rebekah (Genesis 24: 3-4).

Furthermore, Rebekah was so upset that her son Esaus/Edom had married Black women (a Hittitite), that she became sick of living (Genesis 27:46). It disgusted her so much she felt that she would rather be dead! This is offensive to me. I don't know about you, but to me it is very offensive. We revered these people as our prophets and they didn't even like Blacks!

When Moses married a Black woman from Cush (Ethiopia), both Miriam and Aaron spoke badly about him (numbers 12:1). So as you see, these people would rather inbreed then marry Black people.

The conspiracy to destroy the Black race is seen all throughout the people of Seth's folklore. For example, in the Norse mythology, slain warriors were taken away to a vast hall for the slain in Asgard, called Valhalla. Here, they were entertained by Odin, the supreme deity of war and the dead, and the creator of <u>man</u>. And there they would remain until Ragnarok, the day of doom. At which time they were to march out with Odin to do battle with guess who...the Giants!

Herein this glorious myth, we encounter yet again a story of preparation of the people of Seth to kill Giants whom the Biblical text informs us were Black. Also termed the sons of Gods.

Likewise, the Greek mythology speaks of Giants and described them as a <u>race</u> of man like beings of enormous strength and stature who warred with the Olympians, and by whom they were destroyed.

In Greek myth there is a reference made to a giant called Atlas. You may recall him as the person who carried the world on his shoulders. Well, Atlas resided in North Africa. He was the son of Iapetus and Clumene, and father of the Hesperides, Hyanes, and Pleiades.

The Hesperides were nymphs (female spirits inhabiting and animalistically representing features of nature such as woodlands and waters), who, together with a <u>dragon</u>, watch over a garden situated at the west end of the Earth. This garden is where golden apples grow. Ring a bell?

As for the Hyades, they were five daughters placed by Zeus in the Heavens as stars. Likewise, the Pleiadades were seven daughters who also became stars.

"Atlas and the Hesperides" by John Singer Sargent, (1856-1925). Museum of Fine Arts, Boston, MA

These 11 stars were placed, interestingly, in the constellation of Taurus the bull.

Atlas also had a brother called Prometheus who was said to be a demigod, and one of the Titans. Prometheus was said to have stolen fire from the gods for the benefit of mankind. Zeus punished Prometheus by binding him to a rock where each day his liver was devoured by an eagle and each night it grew back.

Now using the symbolism we learned along with cross-references to Biblical text, we can identify a parallel in the stories. Like, with the Garden of Eden. In Genesis 4:16, we read Cain was sent east to Nod upon leaving Eden. Therefore Eden was west of Nod. Atlas' daughter interestingly resided over a garden in the west as well.

The Dragon the Hesperides resided in the garden, which surely parallels the serpent and the dragon of Hermes Trismegistus. Also in this garden, we find golden apples. Thus, we encounter a precious and very valuable fruit, similar to the fruit in the Garden of Eden. We know that the serpent and the dragon are one and the same based on a passage in Revelations; which reads, "He grabbed that dragon, that old serpent…" (20:2). Therefore, this myth references the Garden of Eden. Surely, it is more than a myth.

The Destruction Of The Old World

There can be no serious doubt that the destruction of the Black world order was a conspiracy that was carried out by the people of Seth. For history illustrates the rise of the people of Seth and their attacks against the Children of Ham.

Society defines the people of the world as either Caucasoid, Negroid, or Mongoloid.

Negroid peoples are described as having wooly hair; and yellow, dark brown, or black skin. They include Africans, Melanesians, Negritos, Australoids – such as the Australian Aborigines – the Ainu, the Dravidians – the peoples of Sri Lanka and Papuans.

Mongoloids are described as having straight hair (black in color), little facial hair, yellow to brown skin and distinctive folds of skin over the eyes giving them a slant appearance. These include Amerinds, Eskimos, Polynesians, Mongols, Patagonians, Chinese, Japanese, Koreans, and other Asian groups.

However, based on the melanin in the skin and close skin complexions, there are little differences between Mongoloids and Negroids; hence, they are recognized as the same as Negroes to Aryan Caucasoid civilizations.

While the people of Shem were terrorizing the people of Canaan, the tribes of Japheth had busied themselves on all other parts of the Black race.

When we look at the Far East to the Indus valley civilization known as India, situated in modern Pakistan, we learn from the historians that this land was also considered one of the first great civilizations. It was a land founded by Black people called Aboriginal. These were called Dravidians, which comprise Tamil, Telegu, Malayalam, and Kanavese.

In 1500 B.C., the Aryan people of Japheth invaded India through the northwest mountain passes of the Caucus mountains, and brought with them not only the Sanskrit language but slavery as well. The Aryans destroyed all the ancient texts of India and combined other materials with their own beliefs and called this Hinduism. Hinduism thus took the features of a caste system. The lighter you were in complexion, the higher you were in the social classes. This determined the type of education one was entitled to receive as well. Thus, under this caste system Blacks were kept illiterate and in poverty. They were told that they were born Black because of misdeeds in their past lives.

Since the Aryans had both concealed and destroyed the original text of India, as well as incorporated selected portions into Hinduism, Hinduism has no dogma and is almost indefinable. It has no traceable beginning founder or sources of authority. Instead, it has a myriad of connections (with practices such as magic, which was used by the Egyptian priests called Chaldeans), Animism (which are primitive beliefs where all natural phenomena are held to possess an innate Soul), Pantheism (the doctrines that identify the deity with the various forces and workings of nature), Polytheism (belief in many gods), Mysticism (spiritual disciplines providing direct communion with God through deep meditation or a trance-like state, as well as intuition), Asceticism (renunciation of comforts of society for a life of austere self-discipline), and cult sexuality.

The most common belief to most Hindus is the belief in Brahma, the One that is the all. It is the absolute and ultimate principle, which is the self of all things.

Based on the invasion of India, it became known as the cradle of the Aryan civilization.

There are also the Greeks, who invaded Egypt and crushed the culture, and many other European groups who invaded as well. And in doing so, robbed the land of the secrets of the ancient world order.

The Dutch arrived in Australia in the 1600s and by 1778, Britain had created a settlement called New South Wales, emptying all of its convicts into the land. This resulted in the rape and slaughter of the Black Aboriginal people.

The history of the people of Seth has been written eagerly with pride of the conquest of all the old World civilizations and the destruction of the secrets of the Giants and their true origins. Why would the people of Seth go to such extremes, but for the concealment of their origin, hatred of the sons of God, and to usher in a new World order where the people of Seth rule the world. Today many hate groups continue to flourish and increase their numbers carrying on the ancient propaganda that they are the chosen people.

Who will rise up and defend the Black people against the total annihilation of the sons of God. For on this very day, a proud race of Giants is dying away and there is no ark left to carry on the righteousness.

So I ask you now, in the words of Psalms, "O' rise O' God and judge the Earth."